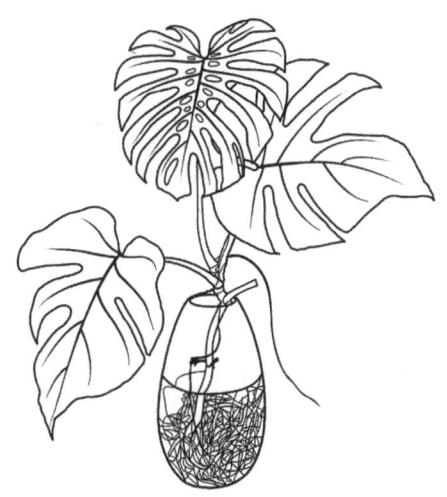

This Book Belongs To:

_____

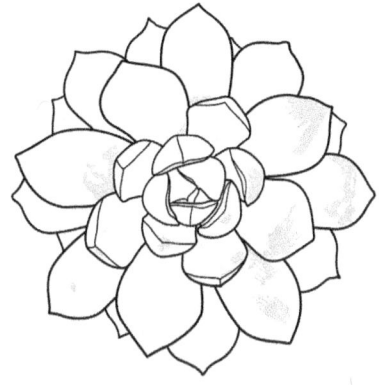

COPYRIGHT © 2020

All rights reserved. No portions of this publication may be reproduced, distributed, or transmitted in any form or by any means, including photocopying, recording, or other electronic or mechanical methods, without prior written permission of the publisher.

Text, illustrations and cover copyright © 2020 Christian Esguerra | Creator of Crazy Plant Guy
Published in 2020 by CSE Marketing & Tecnologies Inc.

This coloring book was designed to be relaxing, fun and interactive. Each coloring page features line art traced from one of my actual houseplants that you can color using your favorite coloring tools. On the back of each page is the name of the plant and an interactive QR code that you can scan using your mobile phone. The QR code will take you to the actual picture of that houseplant that you can use as a coloring reference. It will also include some general information and helpful tips on how to care for that houseplant.

If at any event the QR code doesn't work, or you simply want to use your desktop browser to view the images, you can visit www.crazyplantguy.com/gallery

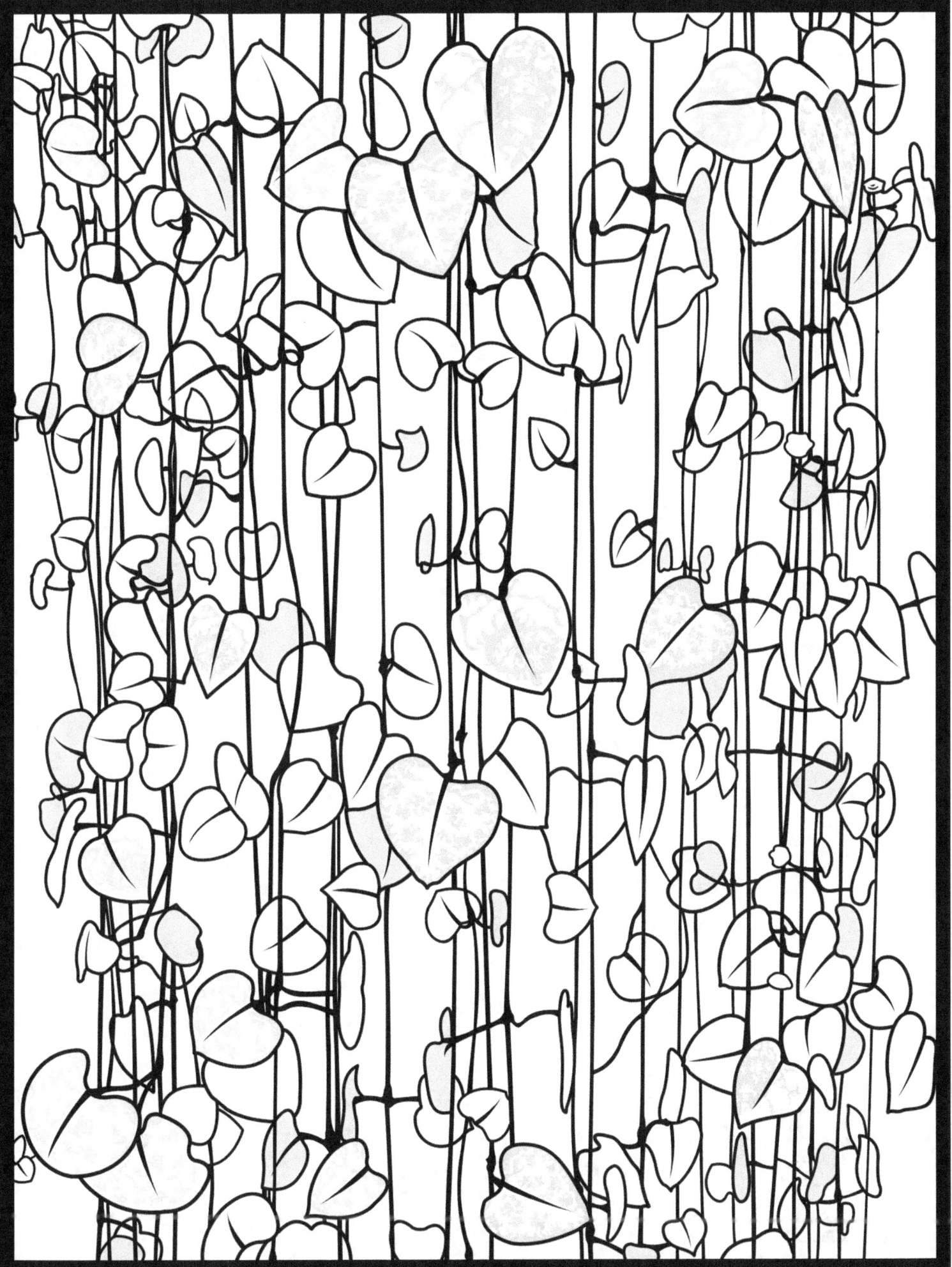

String of Hearts

www.crazyplantguy.com/gallery

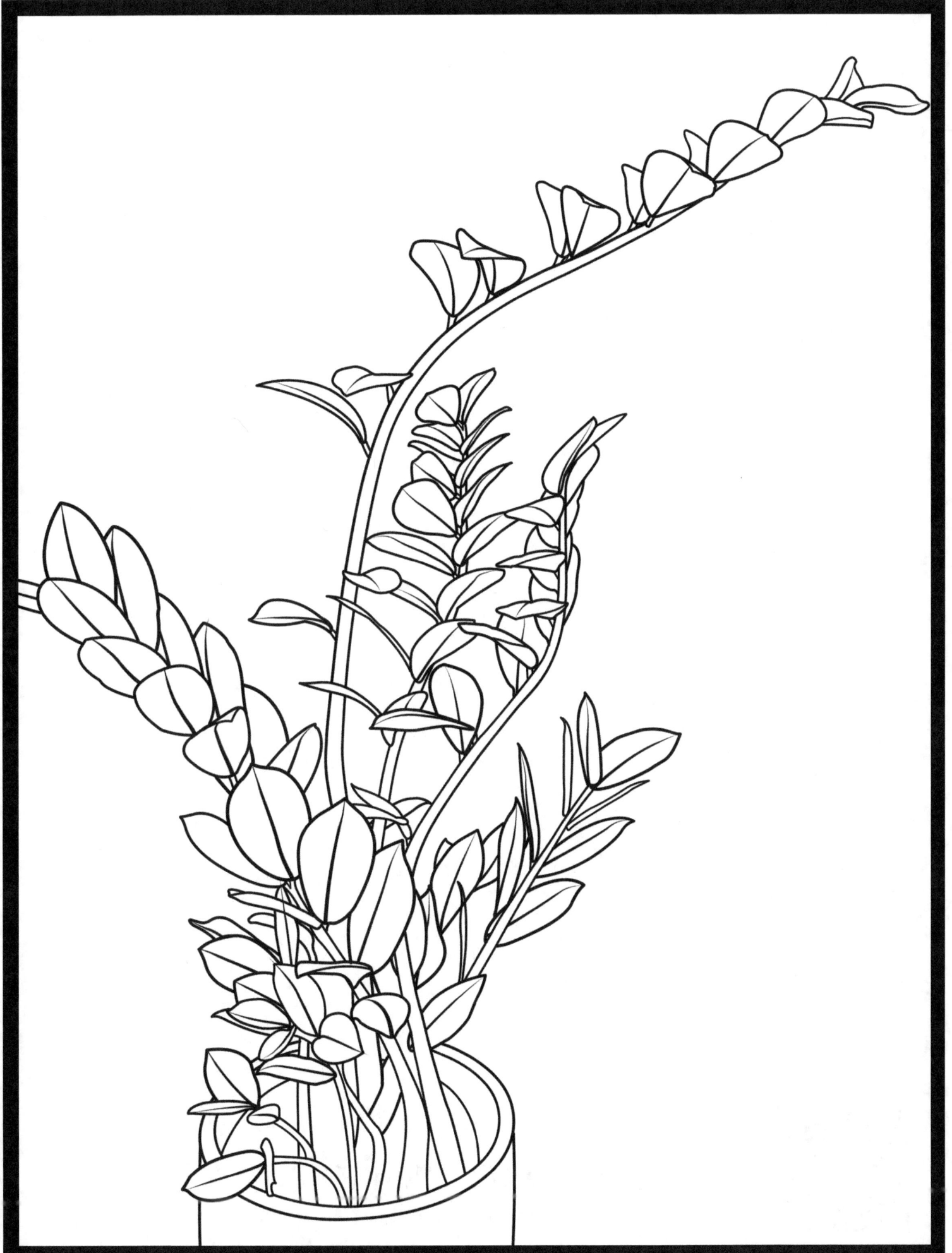

Zamioculcas Zamiifolia

www.crazyplantguy.com/gallery

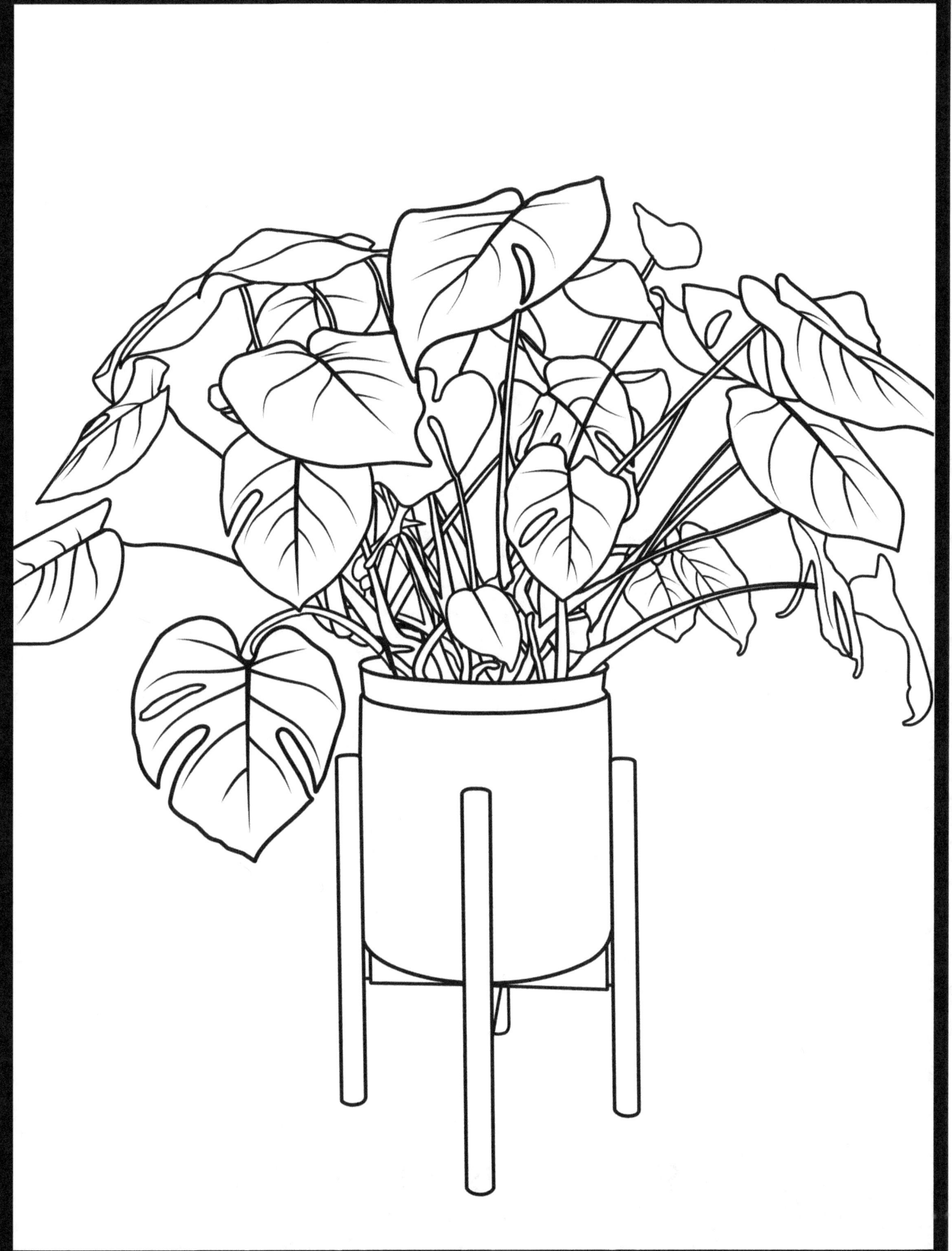

Monstera Deliciosa Var. Borsigiana

www.crazyplantguy.com/gallery

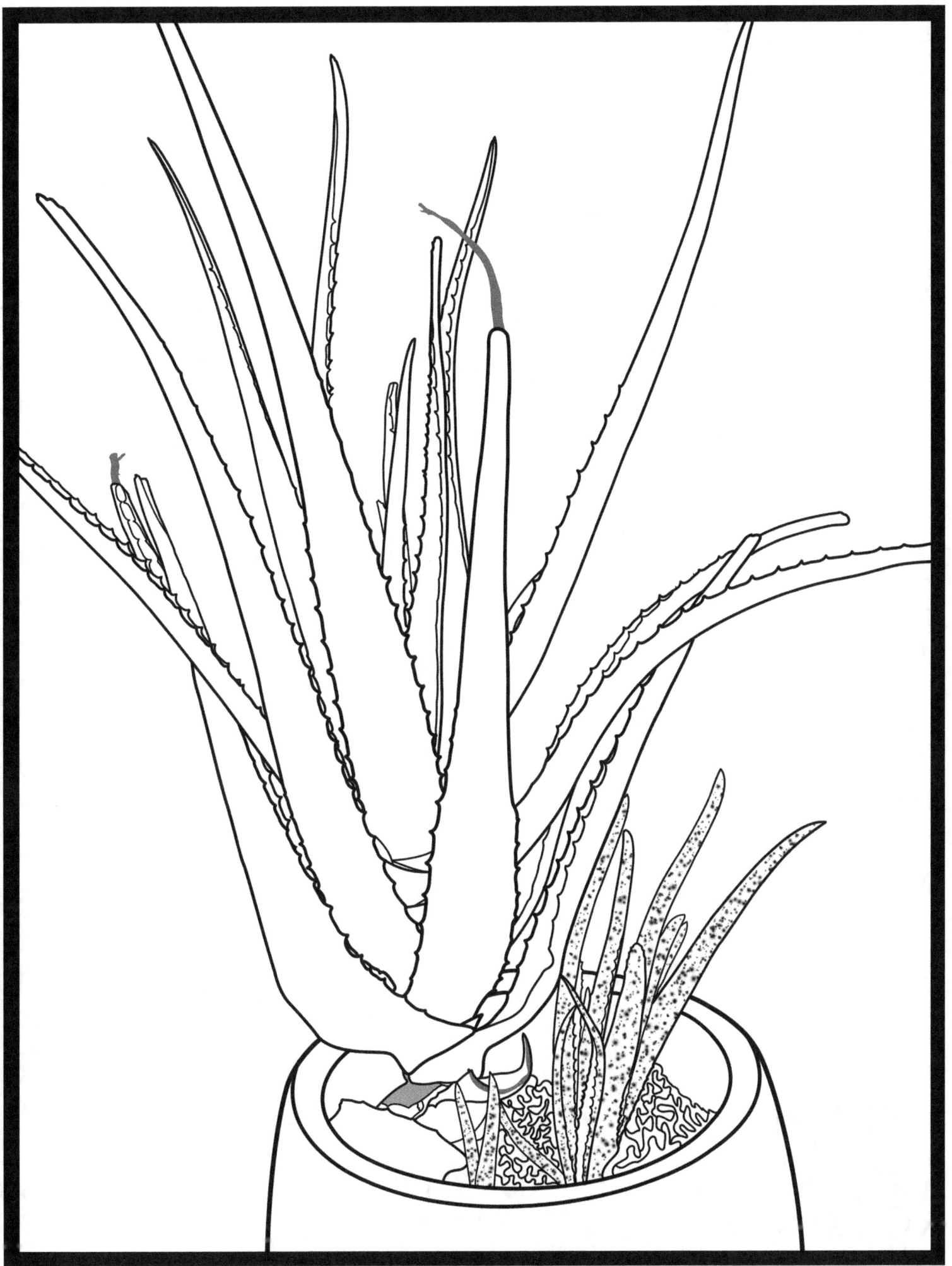

Aloe Vera

www.crazyplantguy.com/gallery

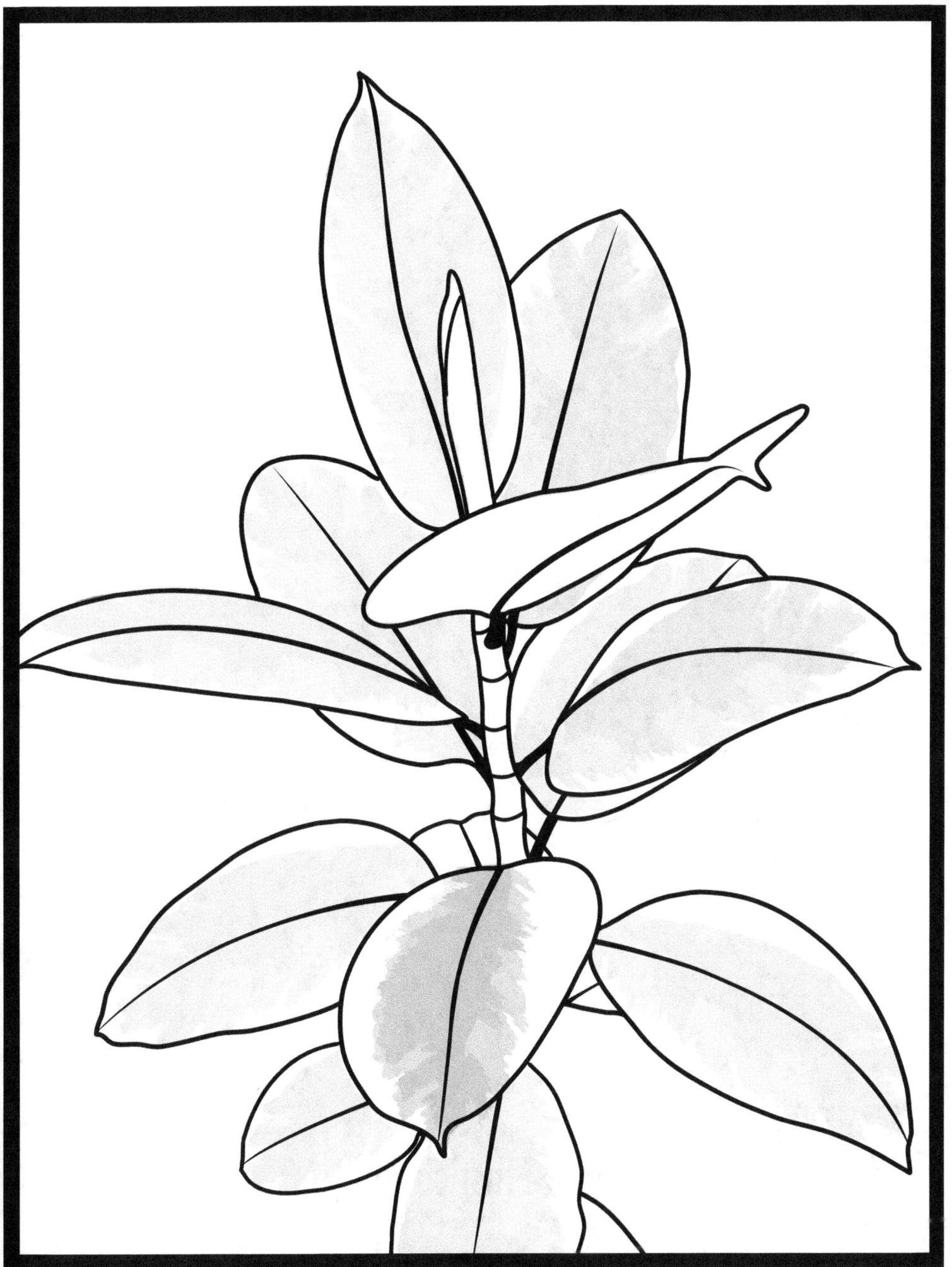

Ficus Elastica Ruby

www.crazyplantguy.com/gallery

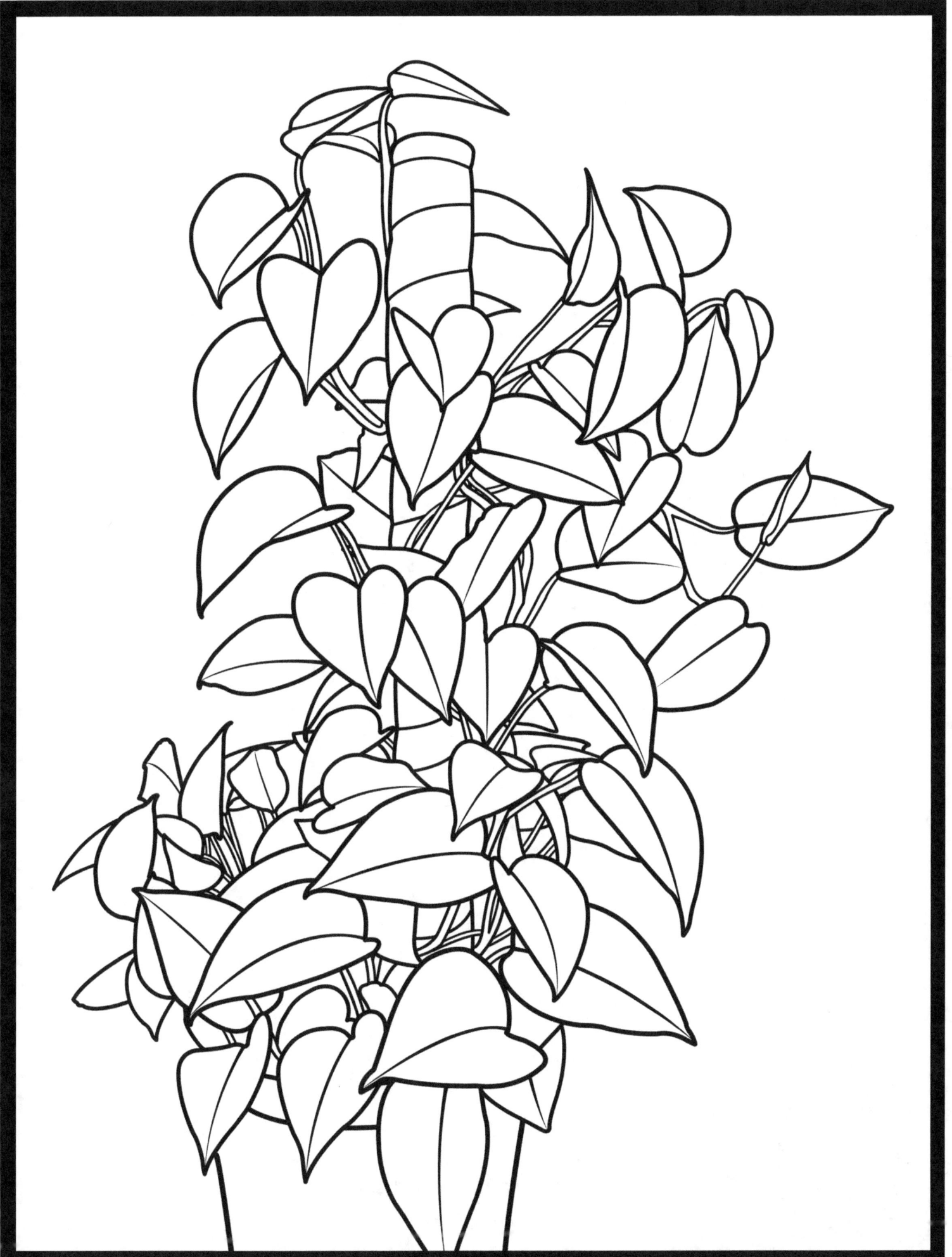

Golden Pothos

www.crazyplantguy.com/gallery

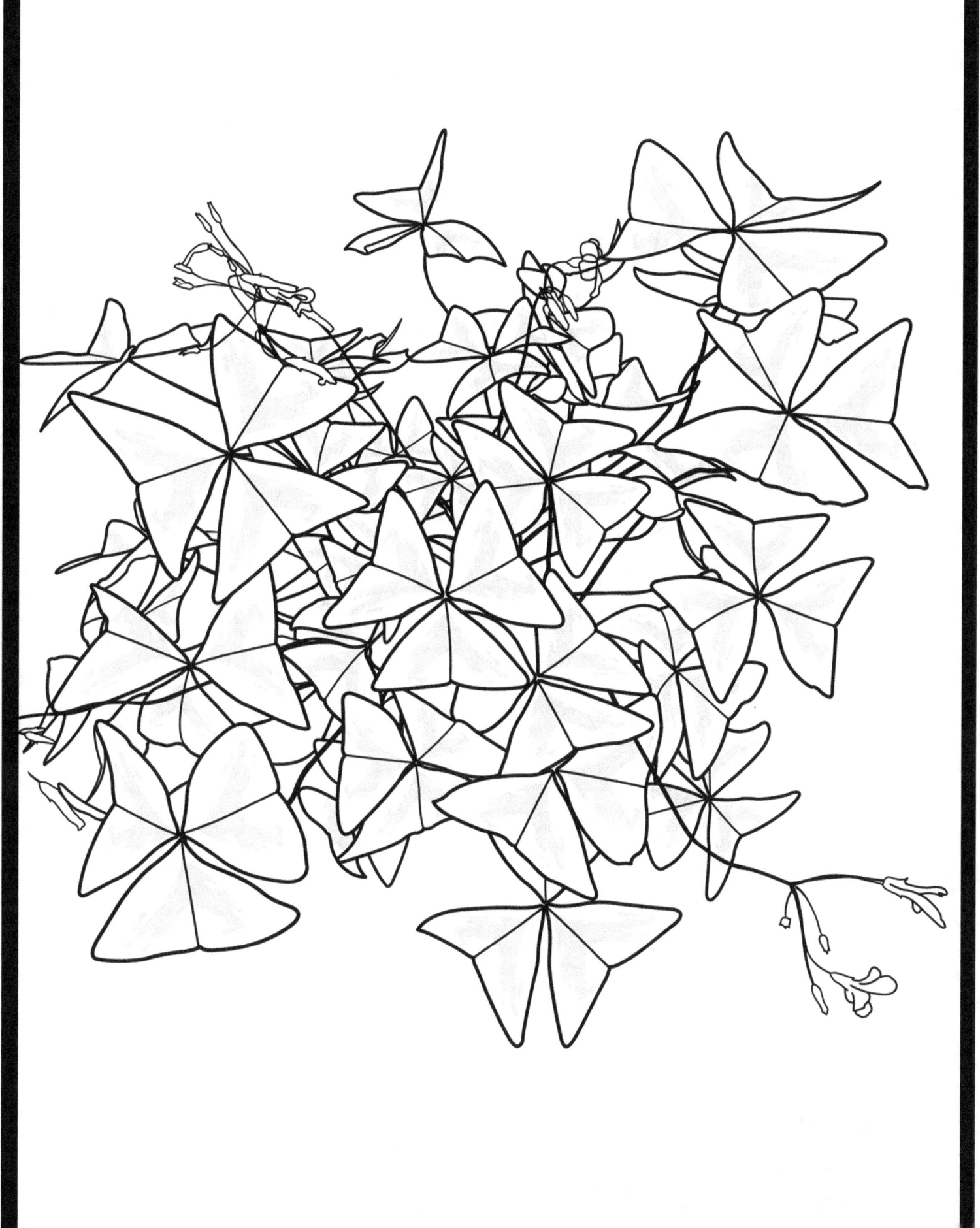

Oxalis Triangularis

www.crazyplantguy.com/gallery

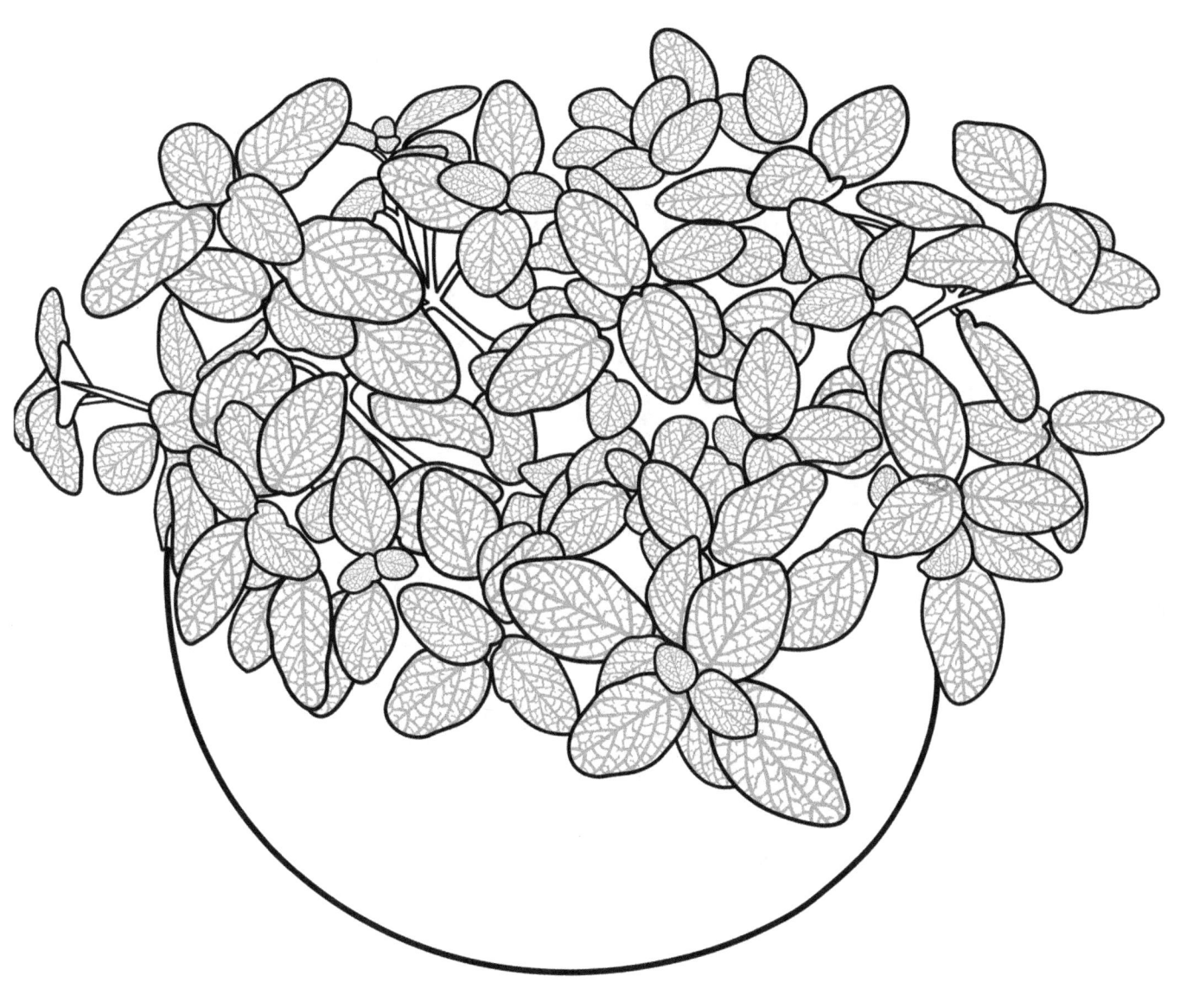

Fittonia Mini White Nerve Plant

www.crazyplantguy.com/gallery

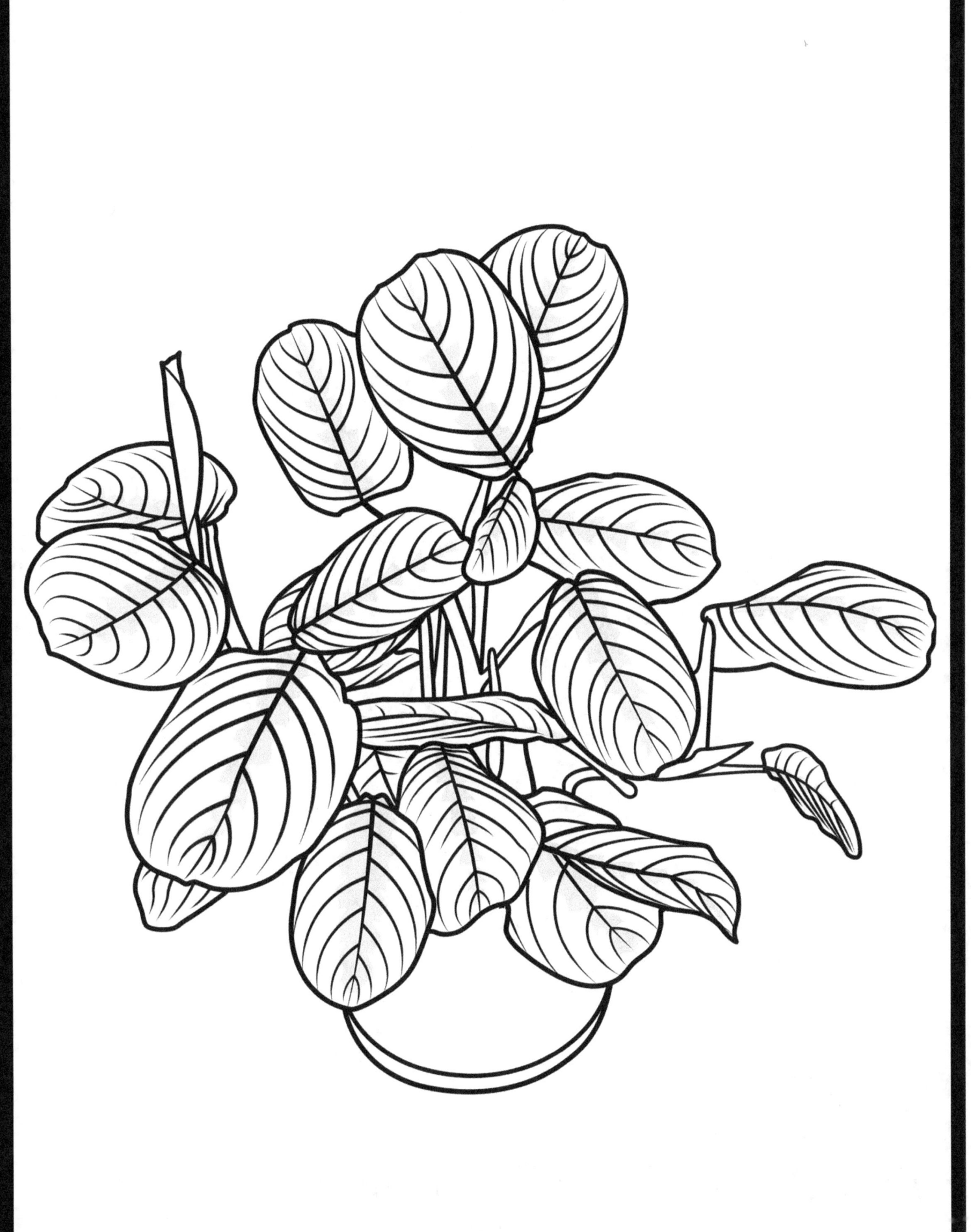

Lemon Lime Maranta

www.crazyplantguy.com/gallery

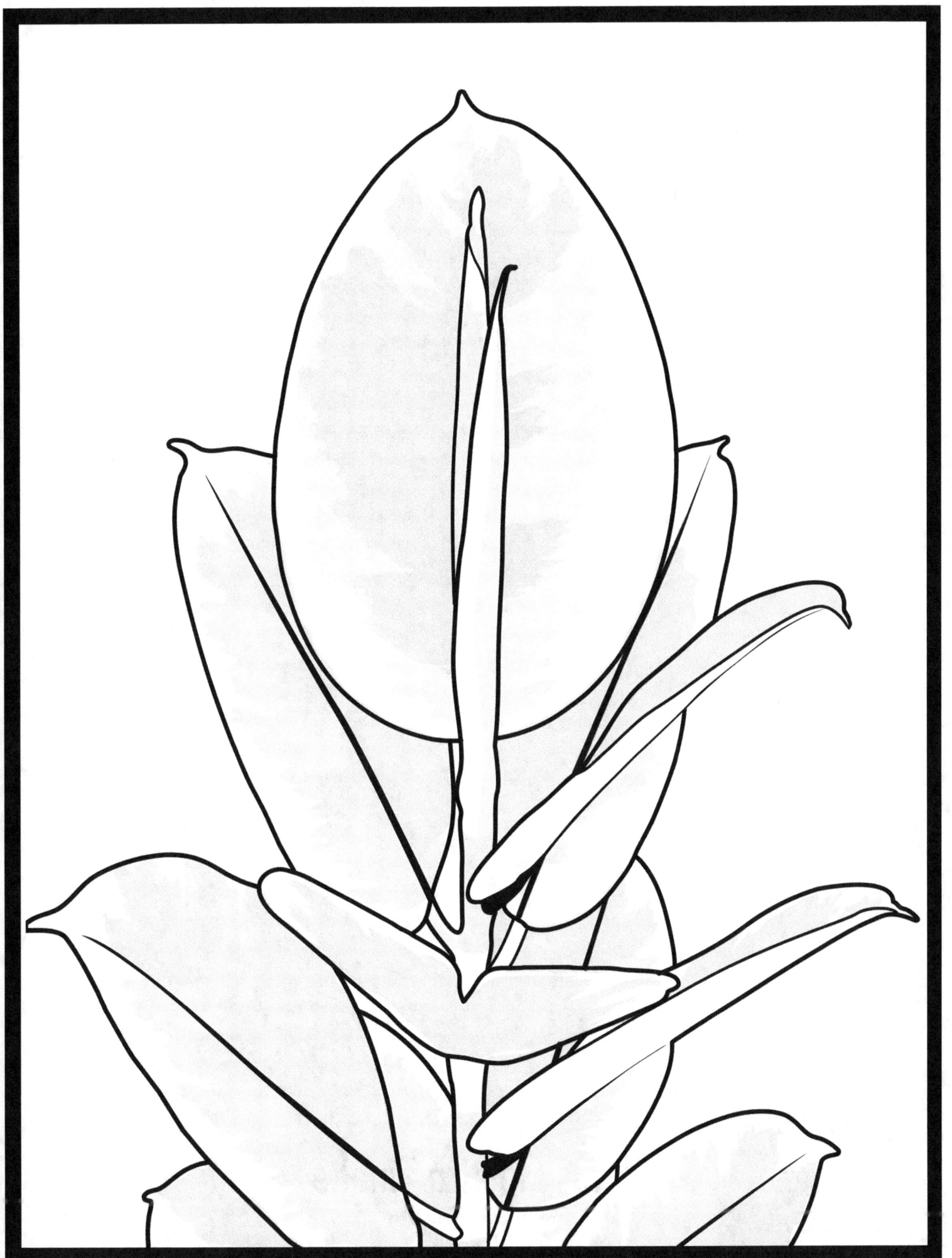

Ficus Elastica Tineke

www.crazyplantguy.com/gallery

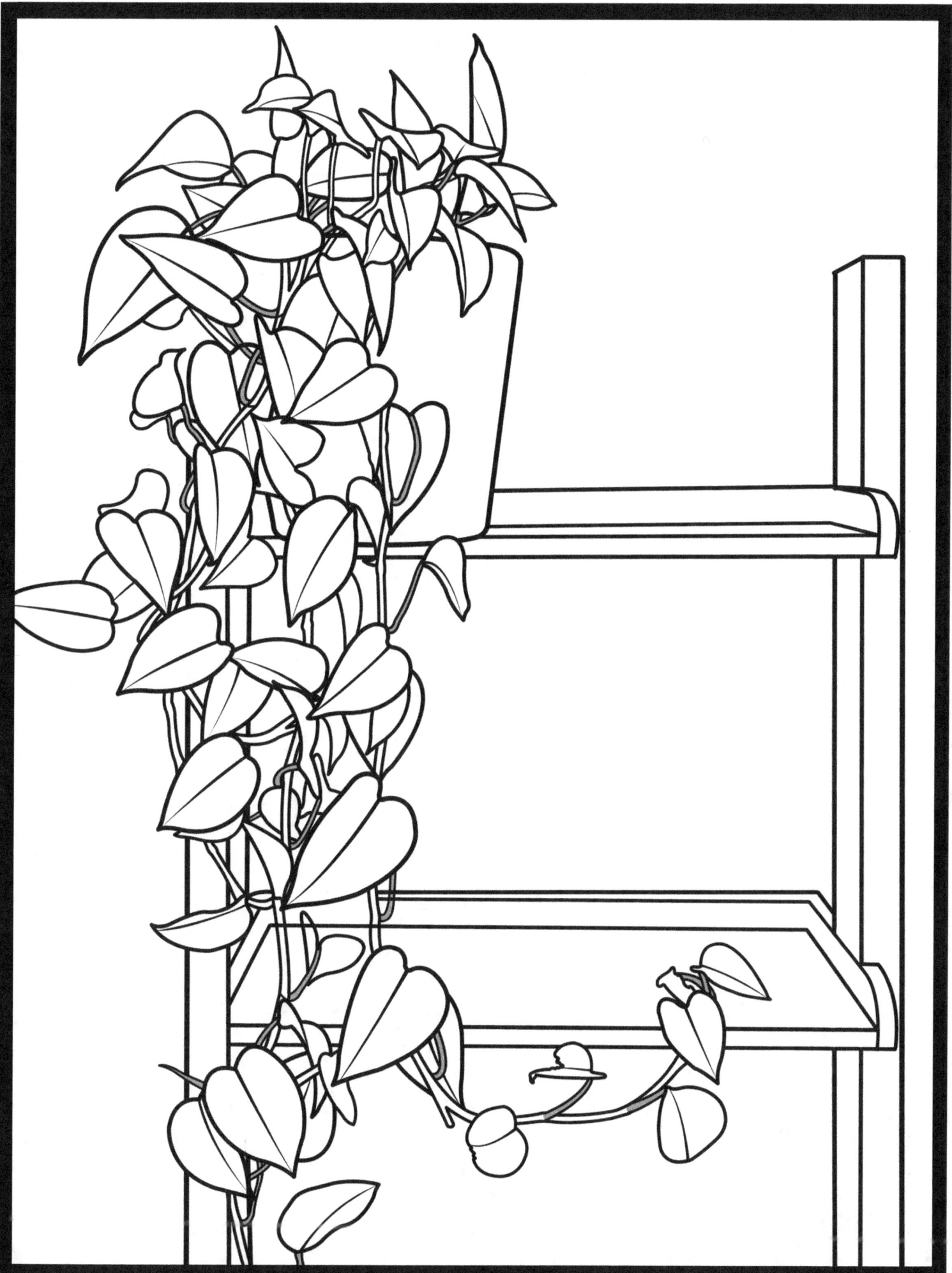

Neon Pothos

www.crazyplantguy.com/gallery

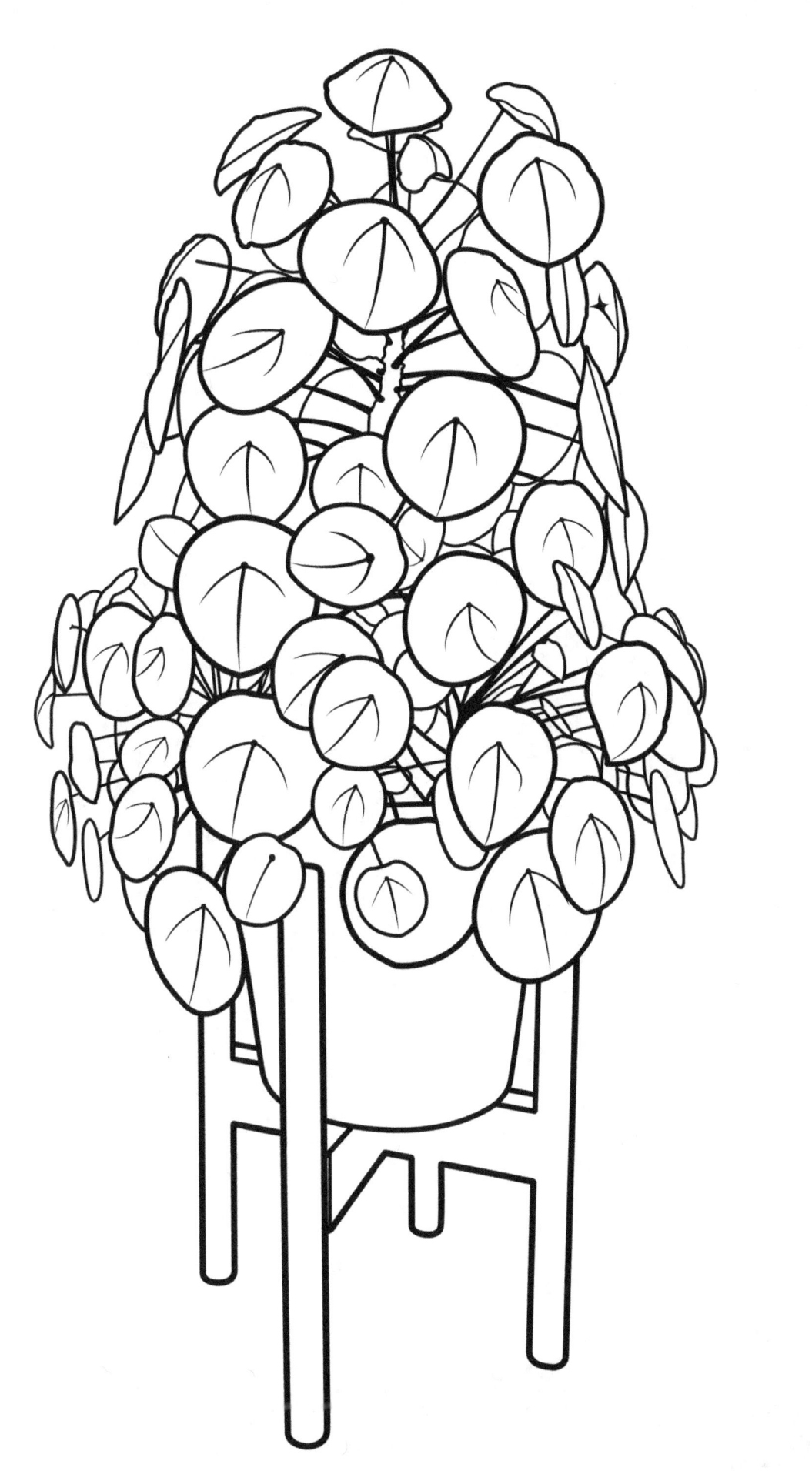

Pilea Peperomioides

www.crazyplantguy.com/gallery

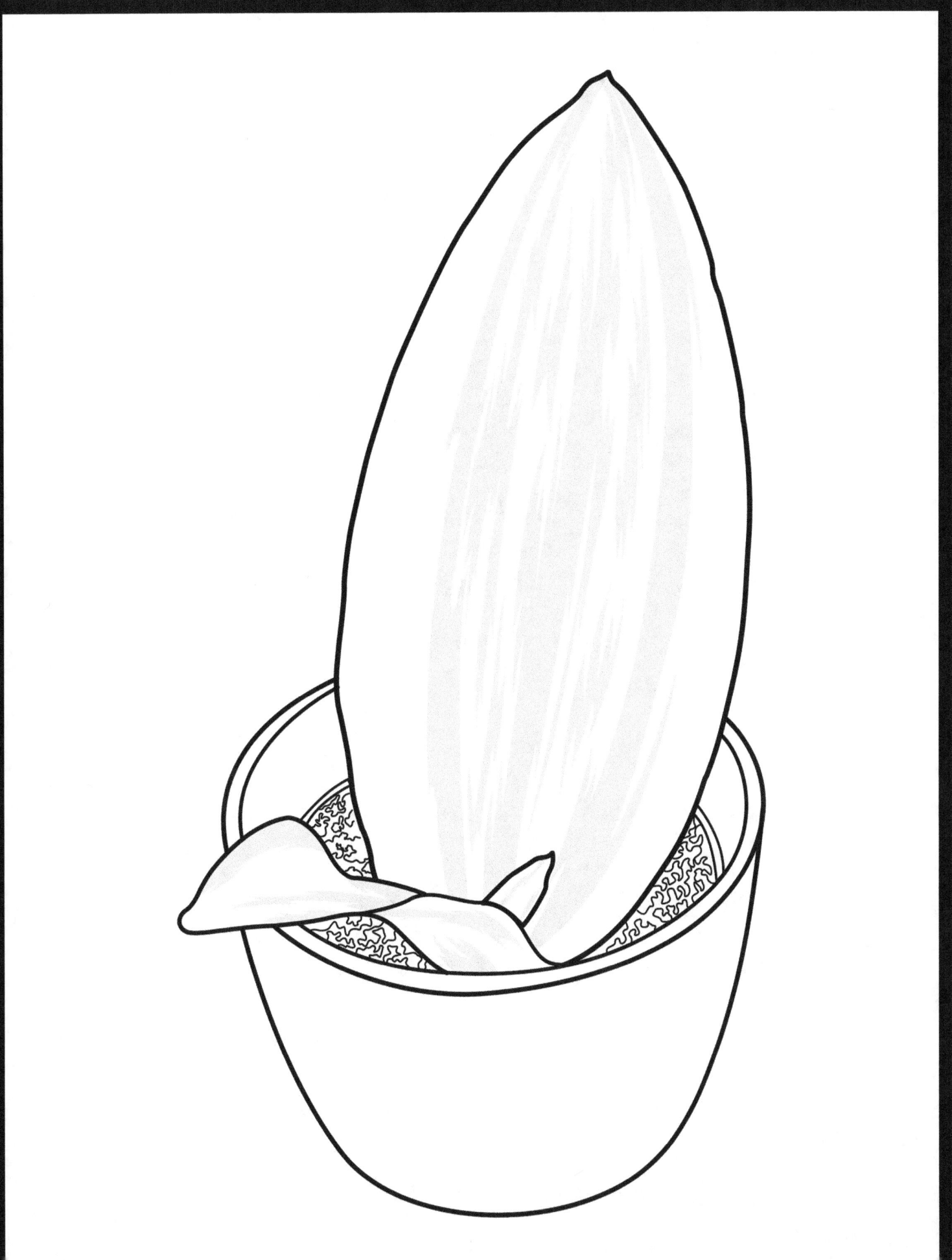

Whale Fin Snake Plant

www.crazyplantguy.com/gallery

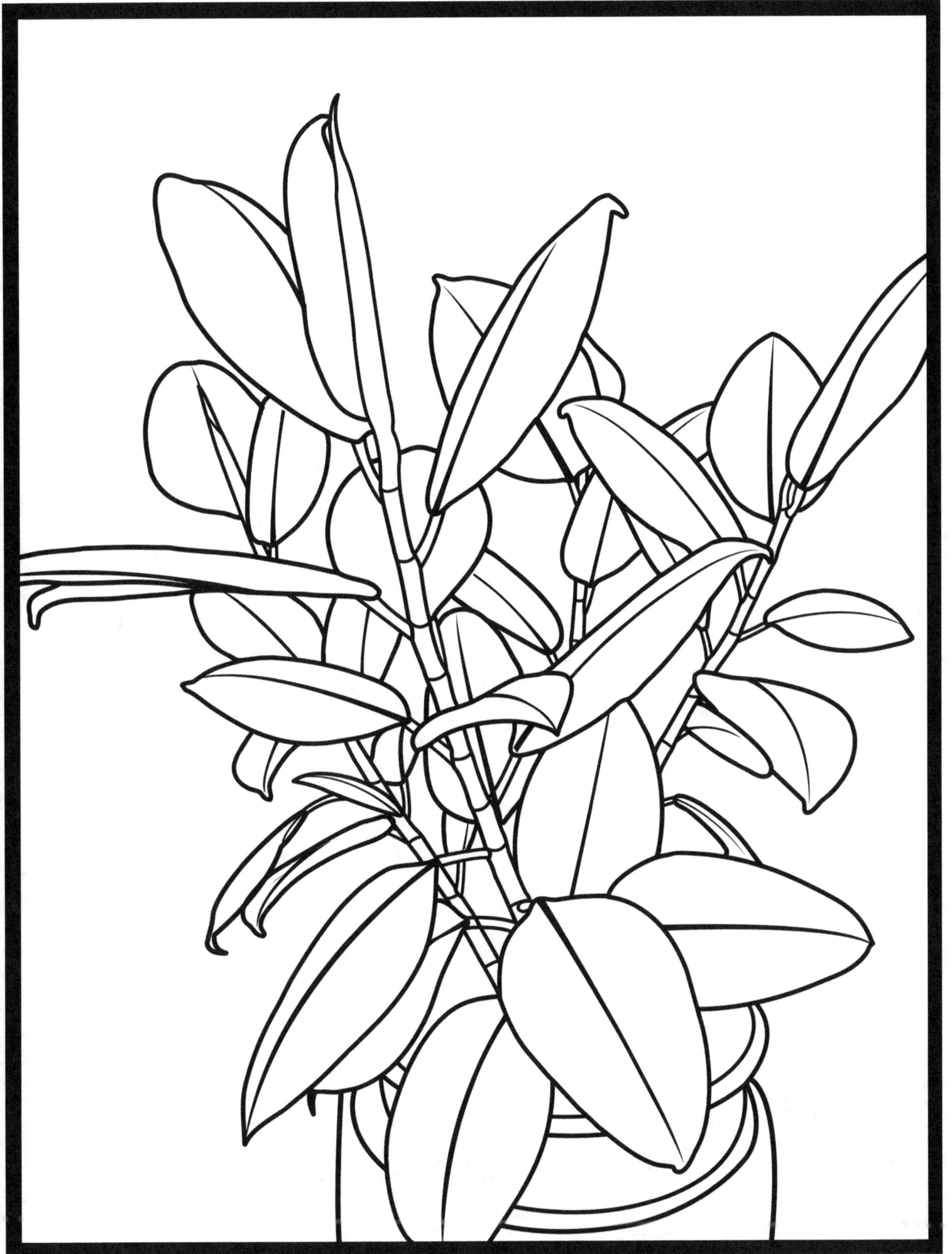

Ficus Elastica Burgundy

www.crazyplantguy.com/gallery

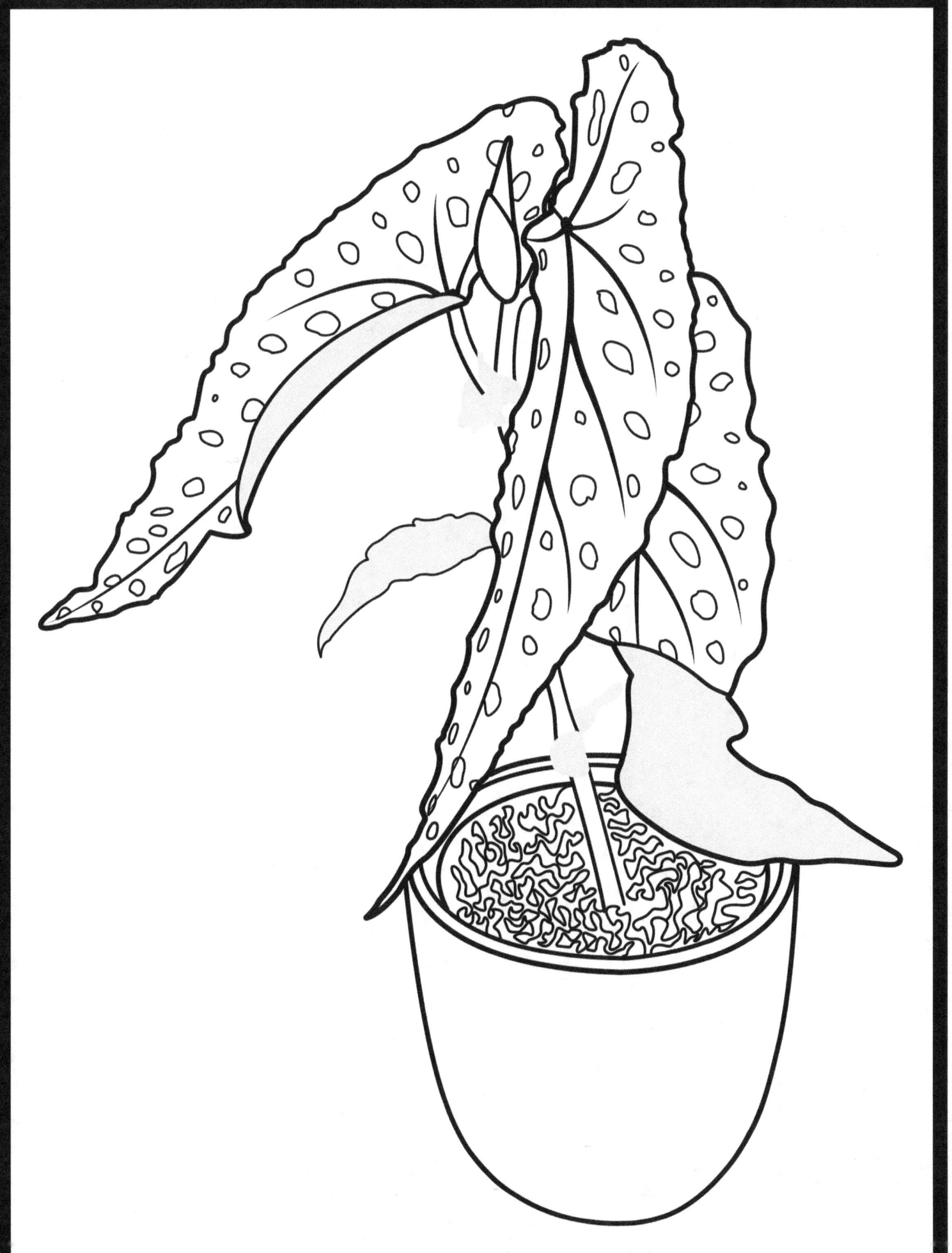

Begonia Angel Wing Maculata

www.crazyplantguy.com/gallery

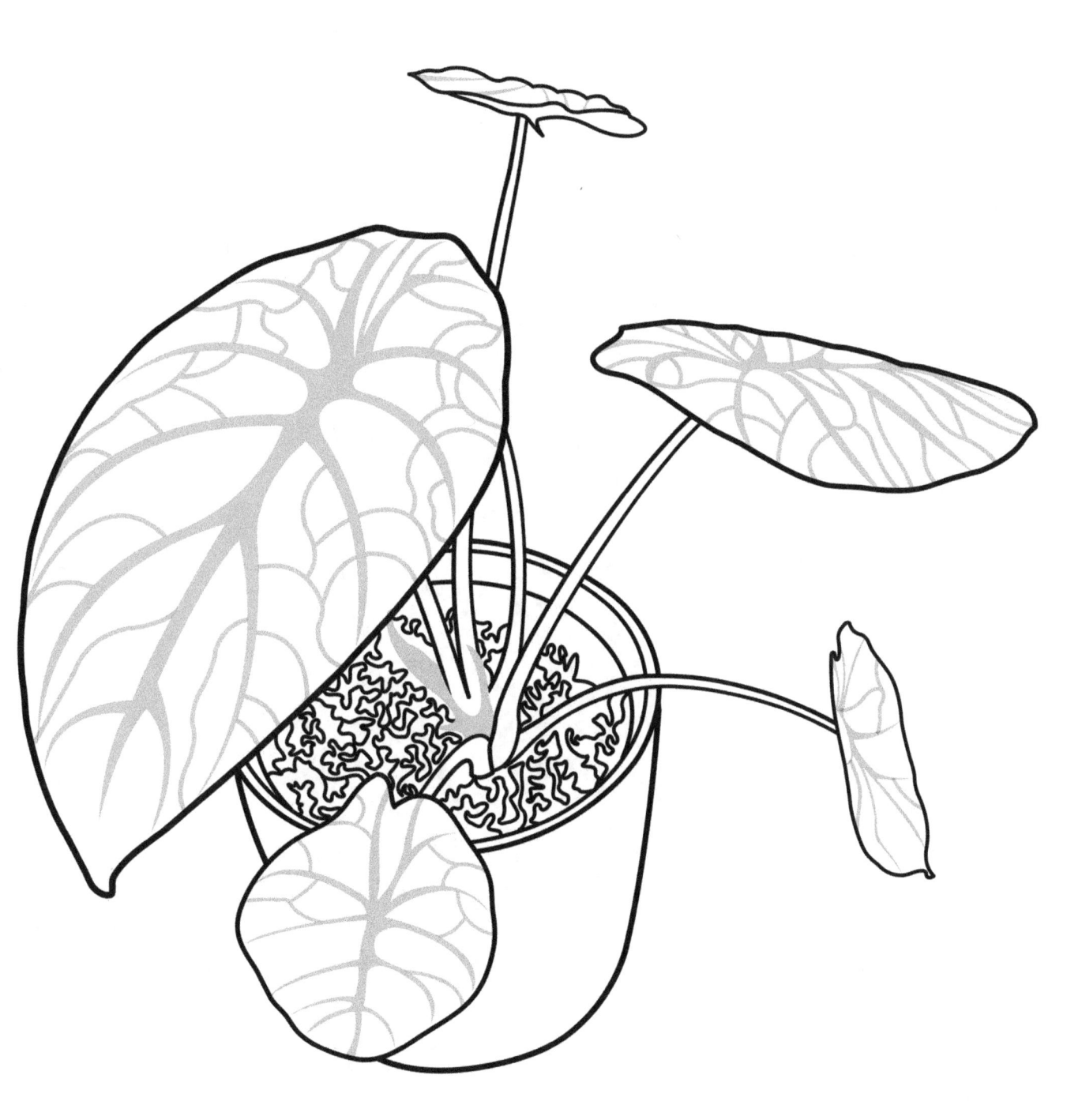

Alocasia Silver Dragon

www.crazyplantguy.com/gallery

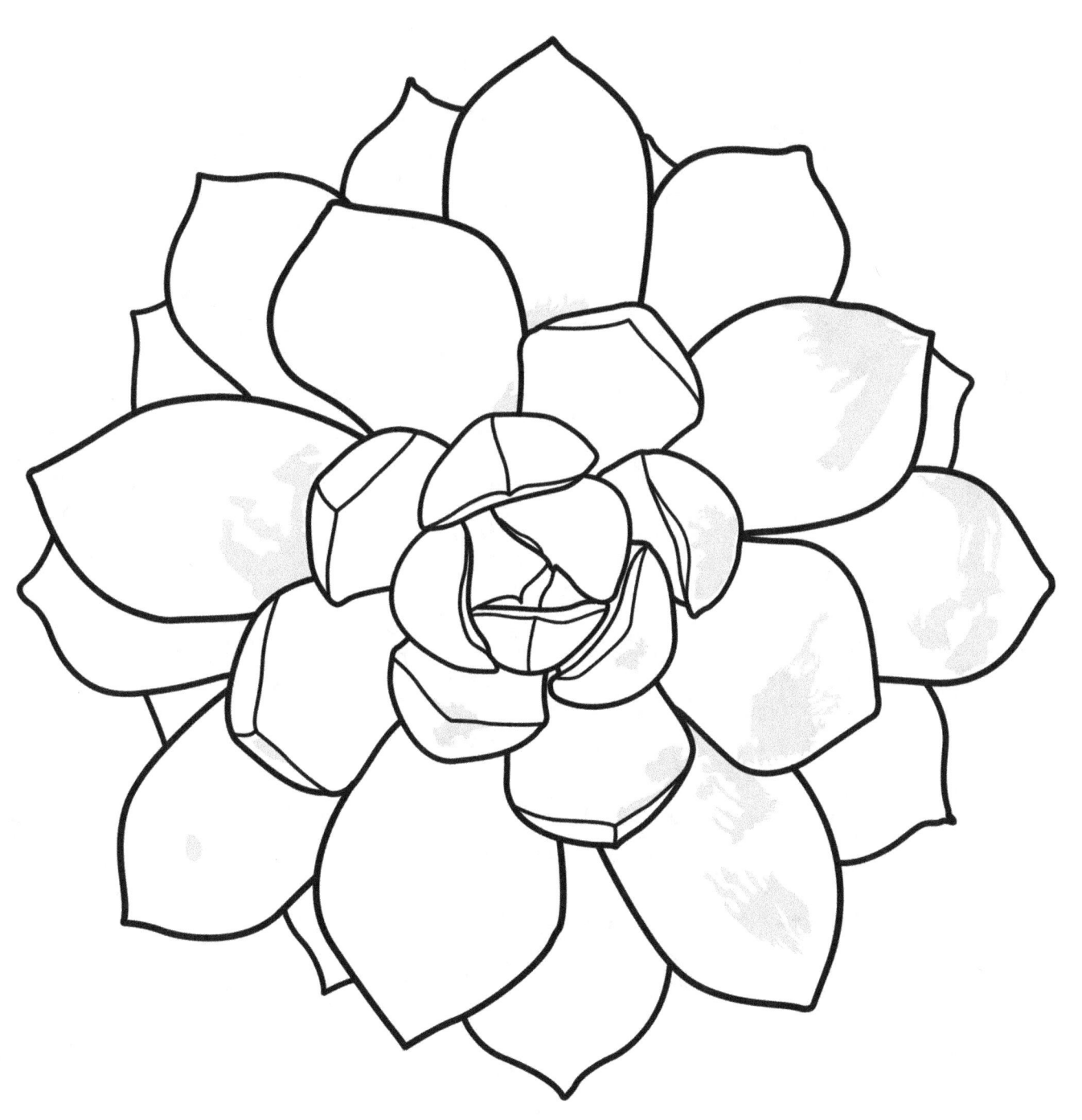

Echeveria Snow Bunny

www.crazyplantguy.com/gallery

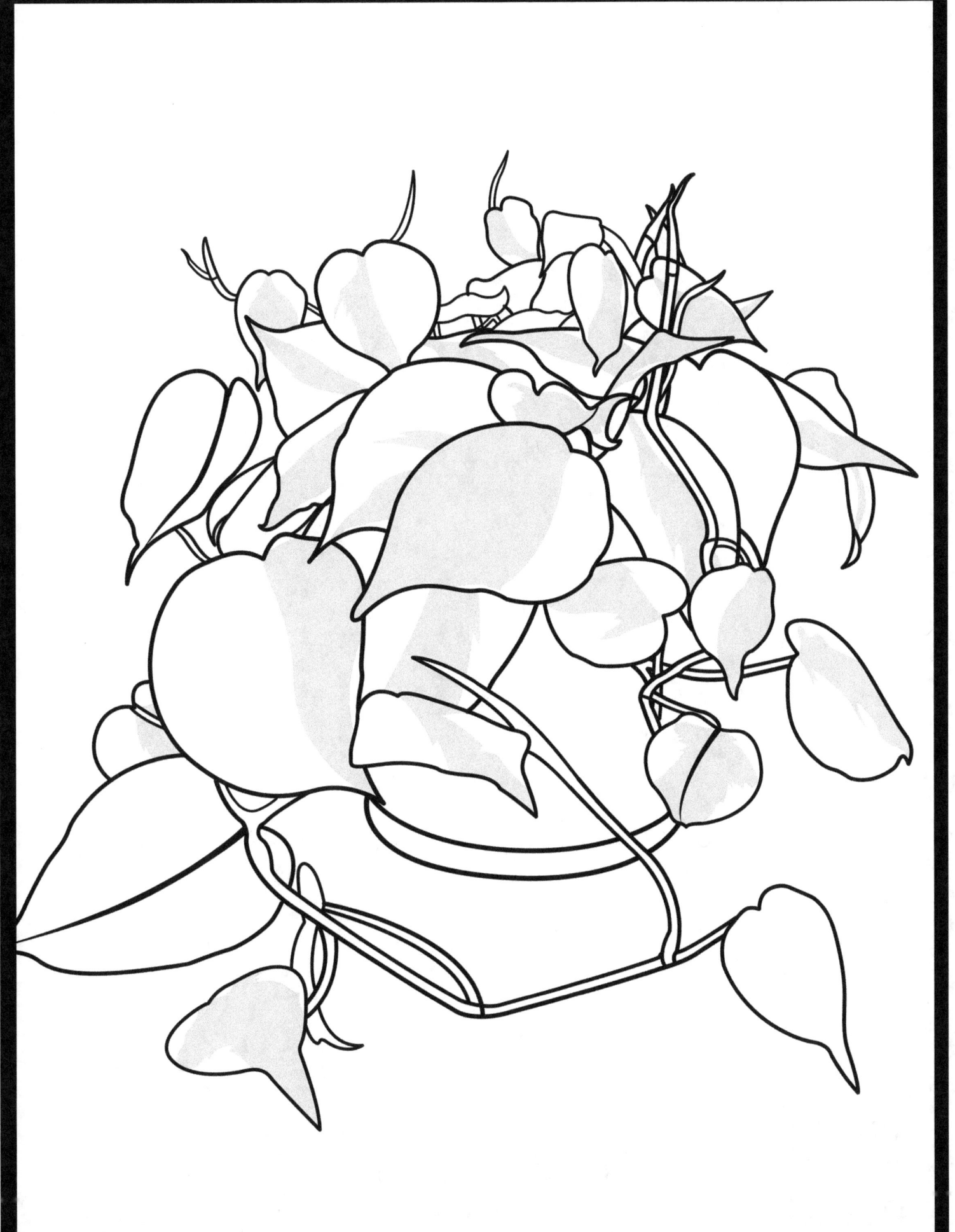

Philodendron Brasil

www.crazyplantguy.com/gallery

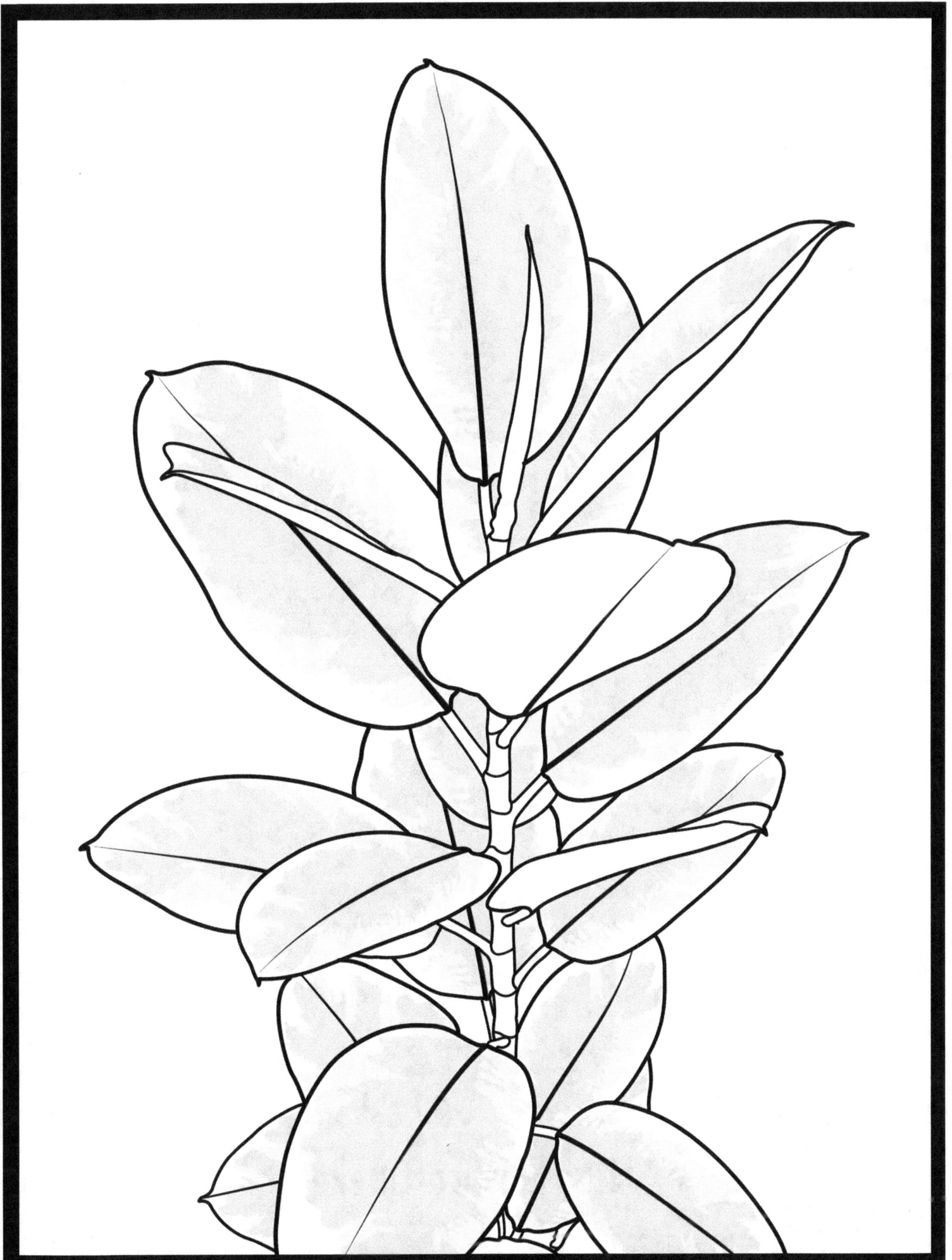

Ficus Elastica Tineke

www.crazyplantguy.com/gallery

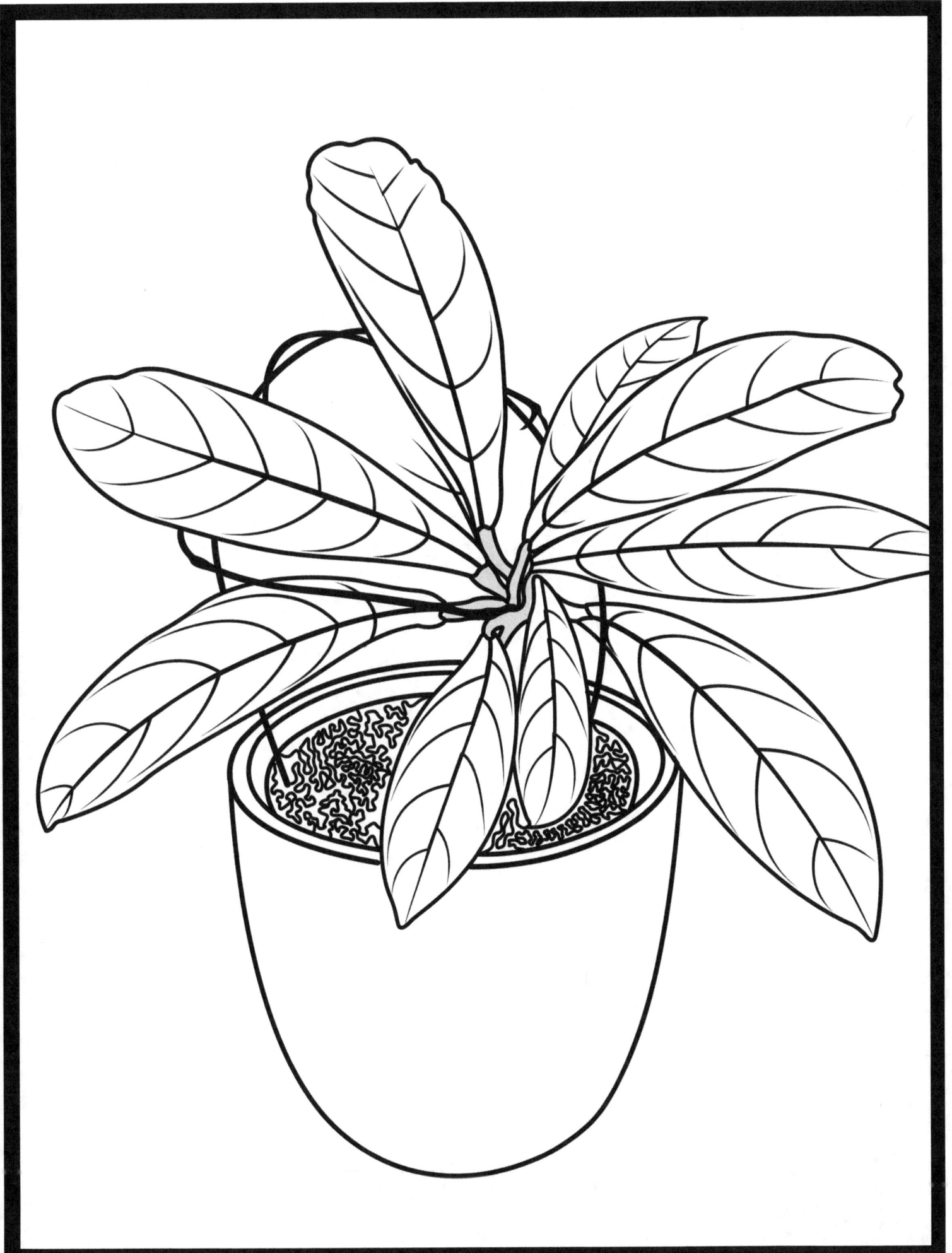

Hoya sp. Vietnam

www.crazyplantguy.com/gallery

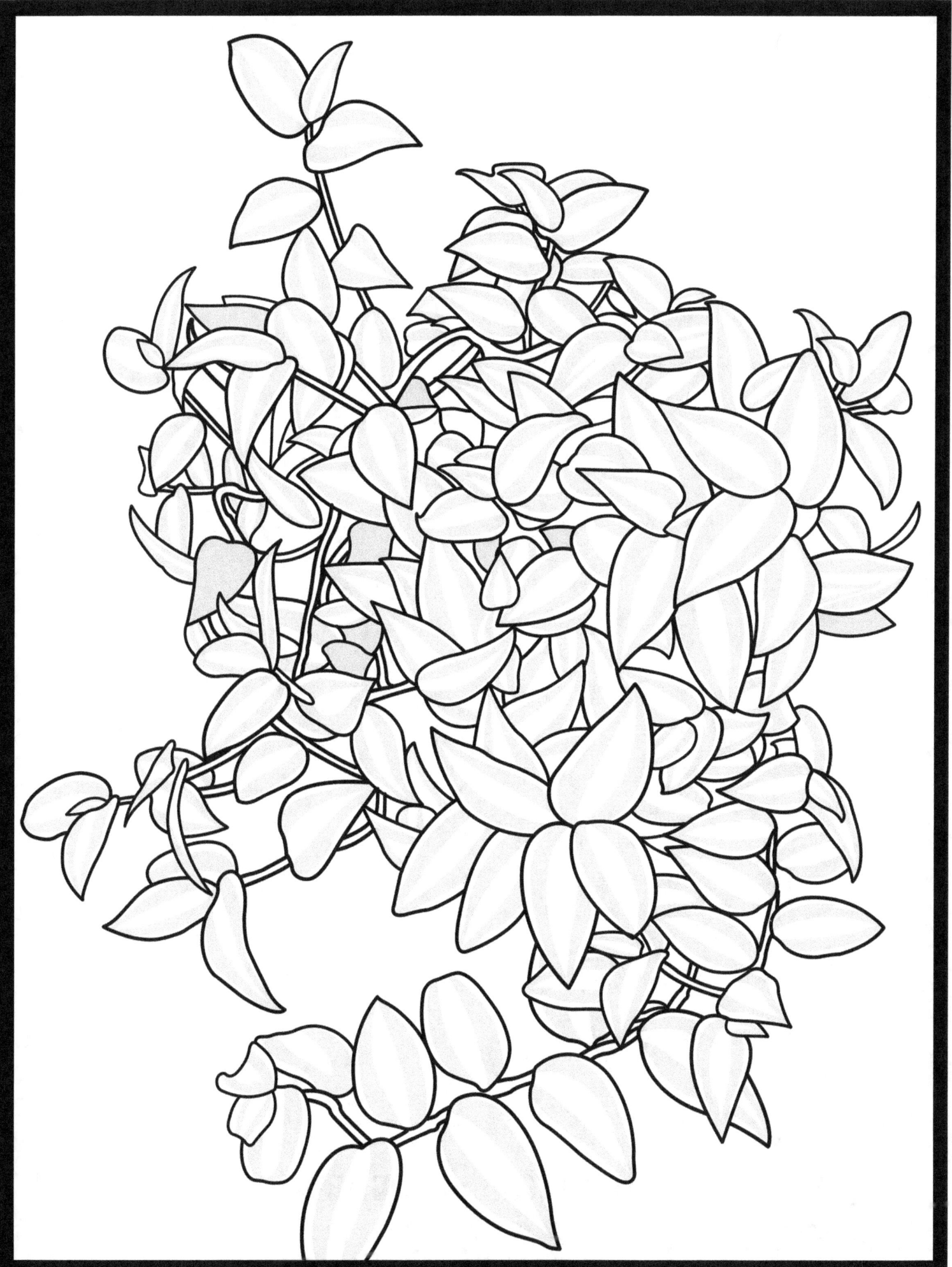

Tradescantia Zebrina

www.crazyplantguy.com/gallery

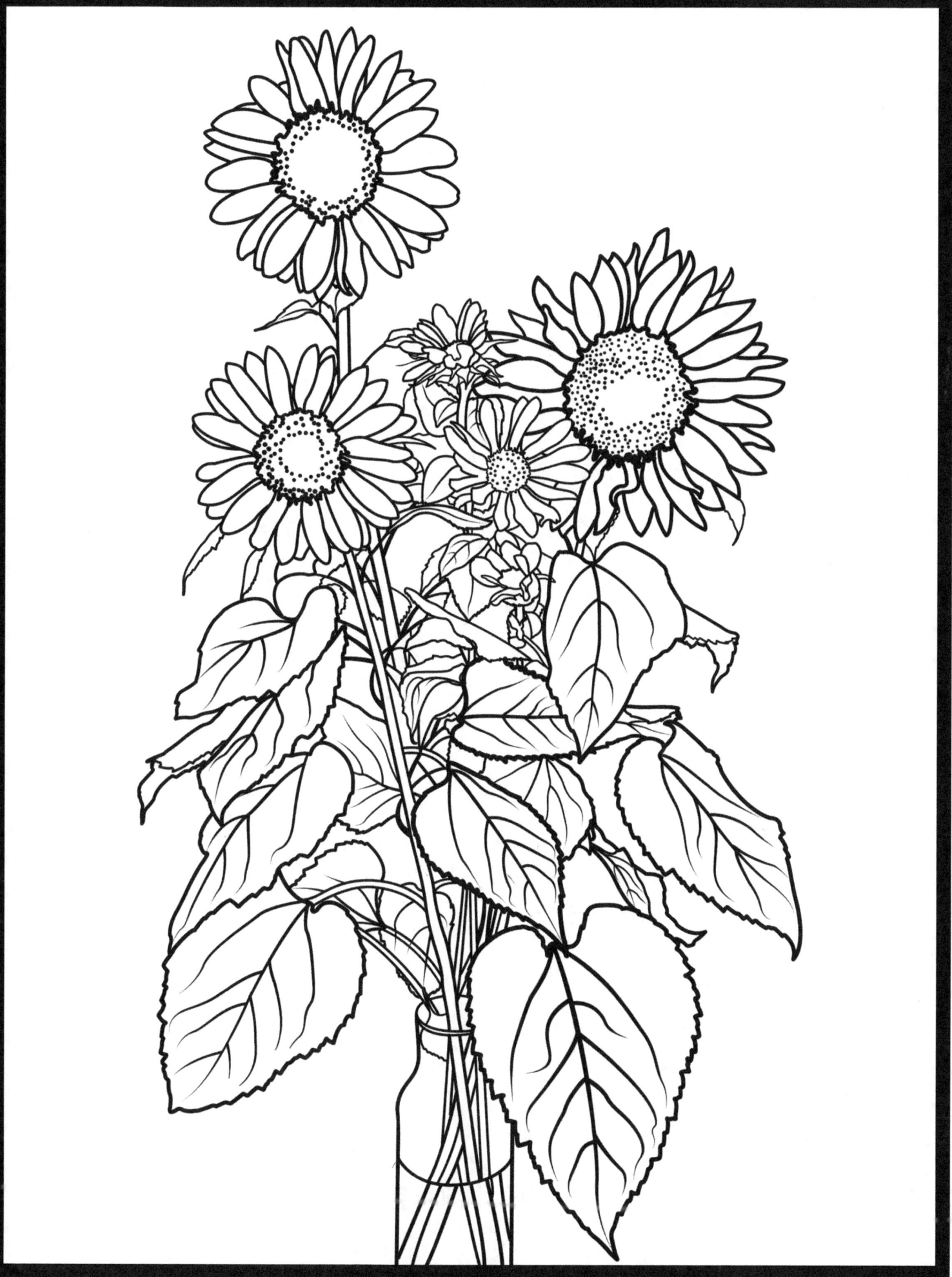

Sunflowers

www.crazyplantguy.com/gallery

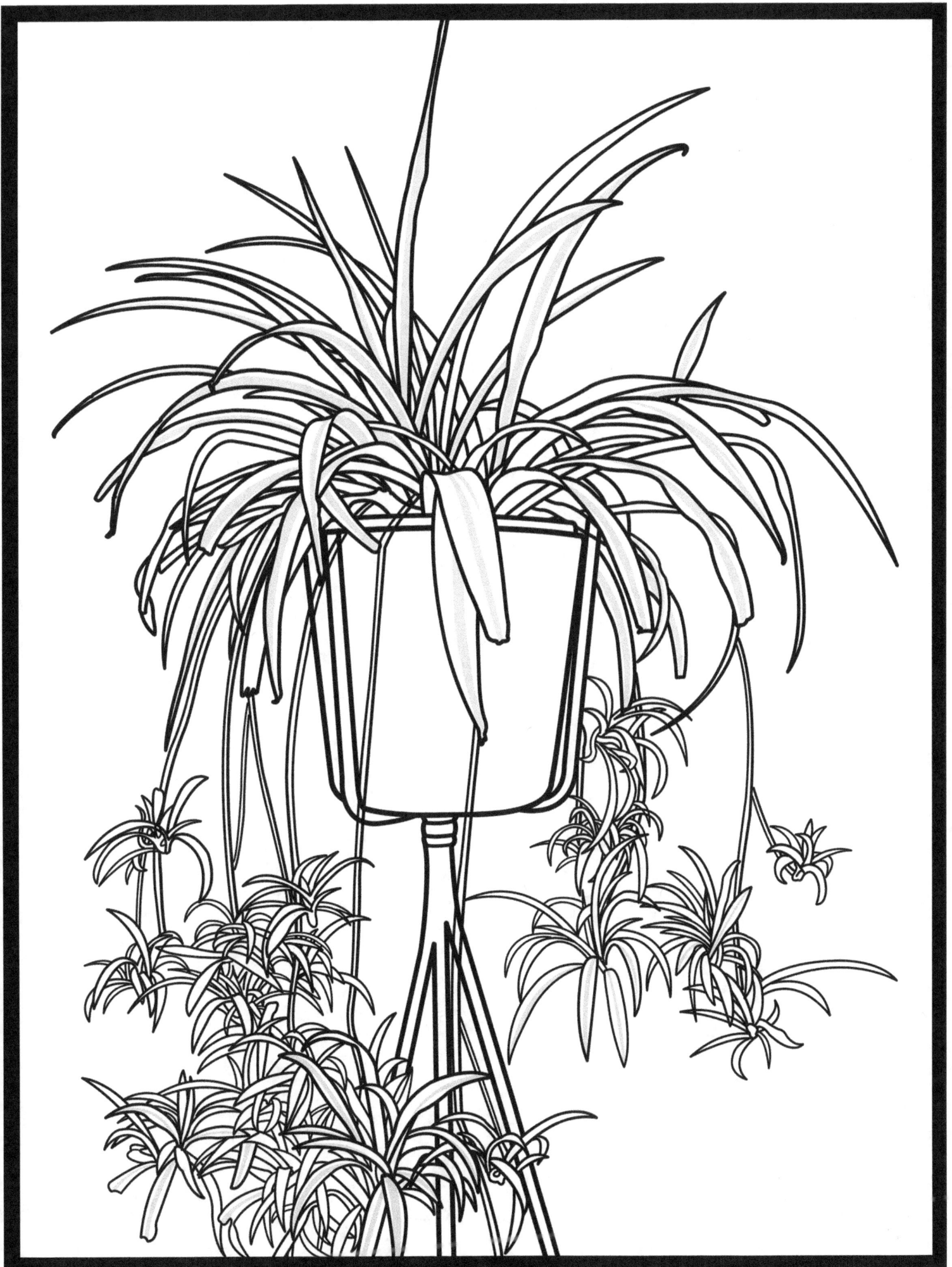

Spider Plant
www.crazyplantguy.com/gallery

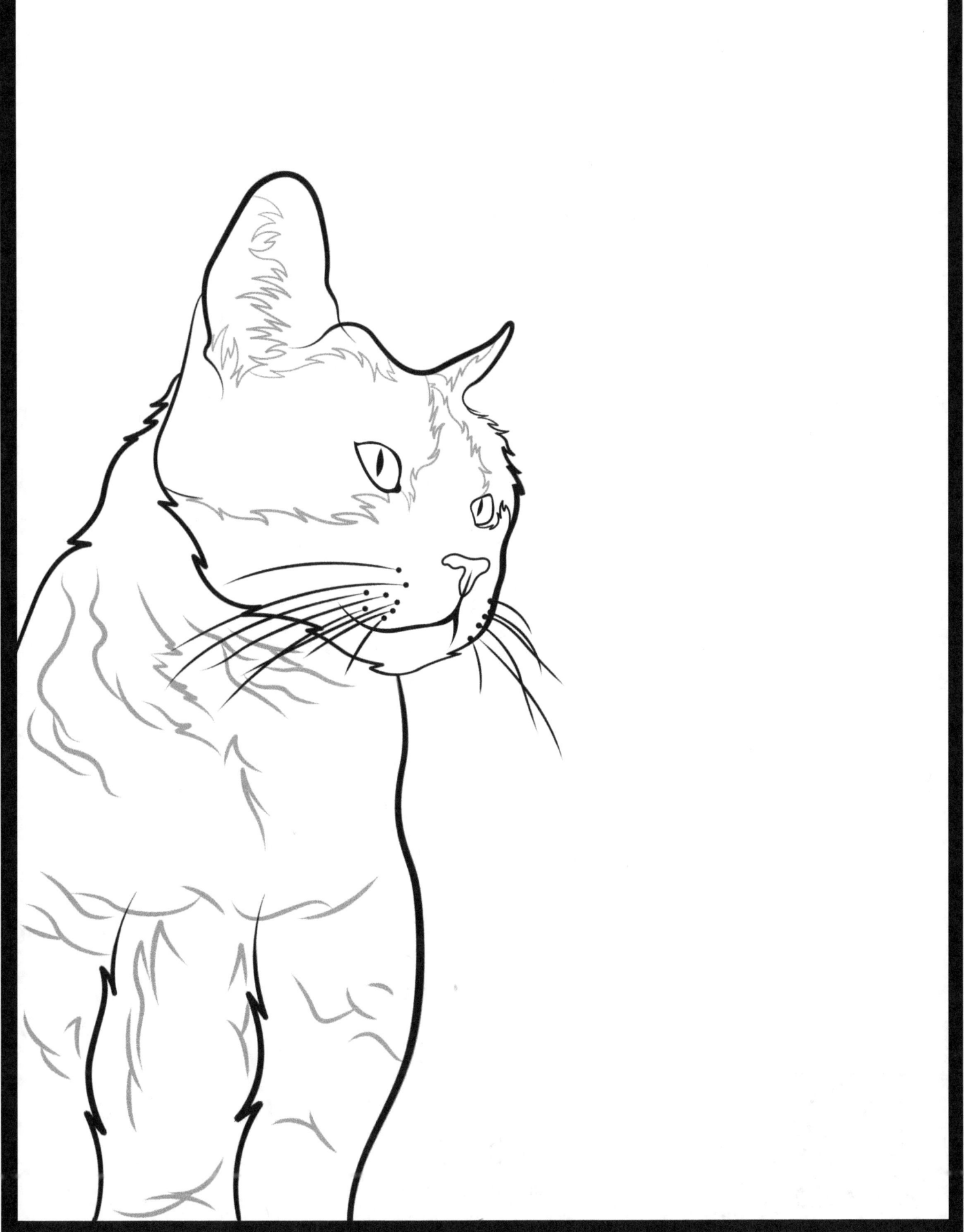

Nemo

www.crazyplantguy.com/gallery

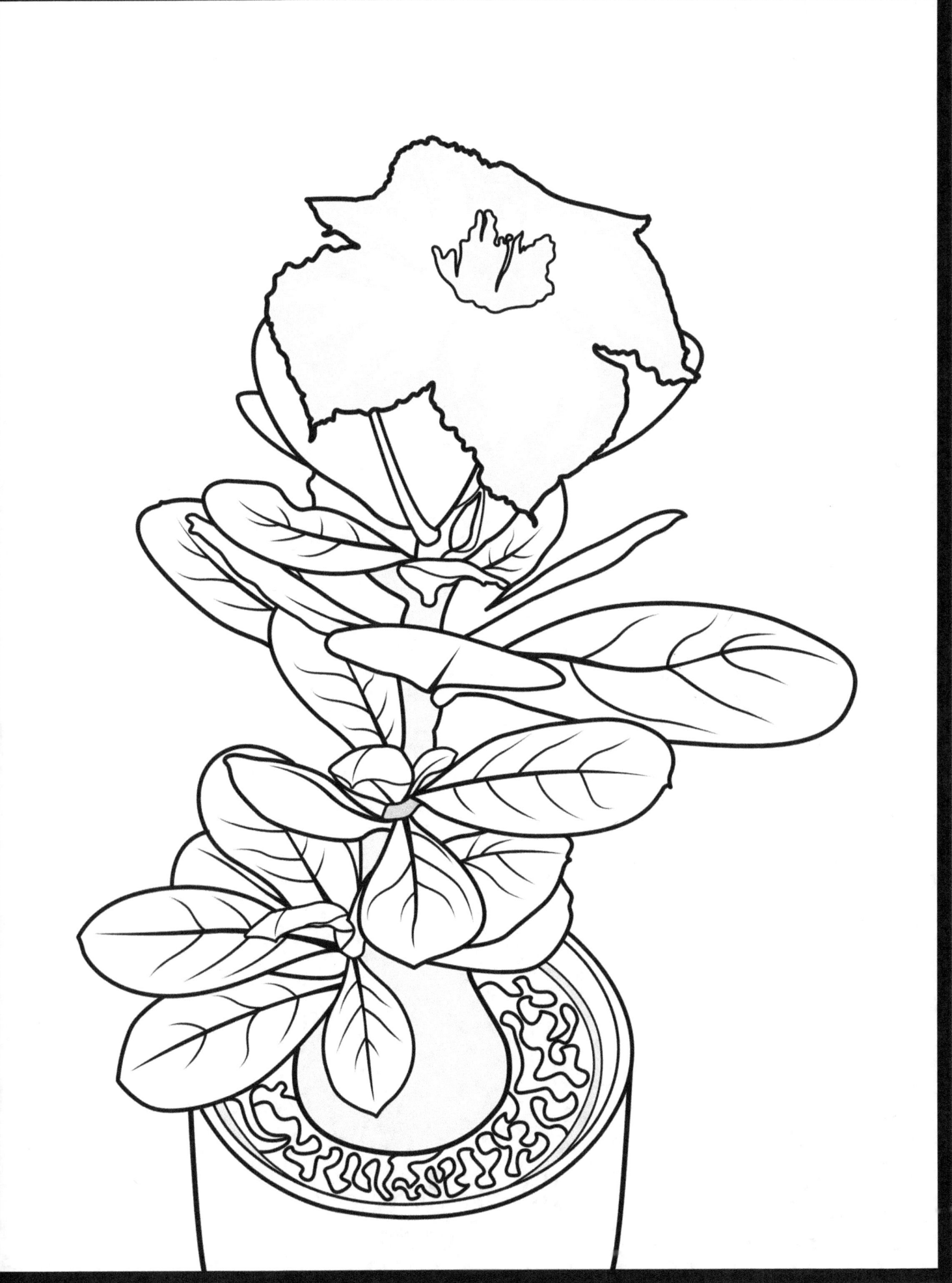

Desert Rose

www.crazyplantguy.com/gallery

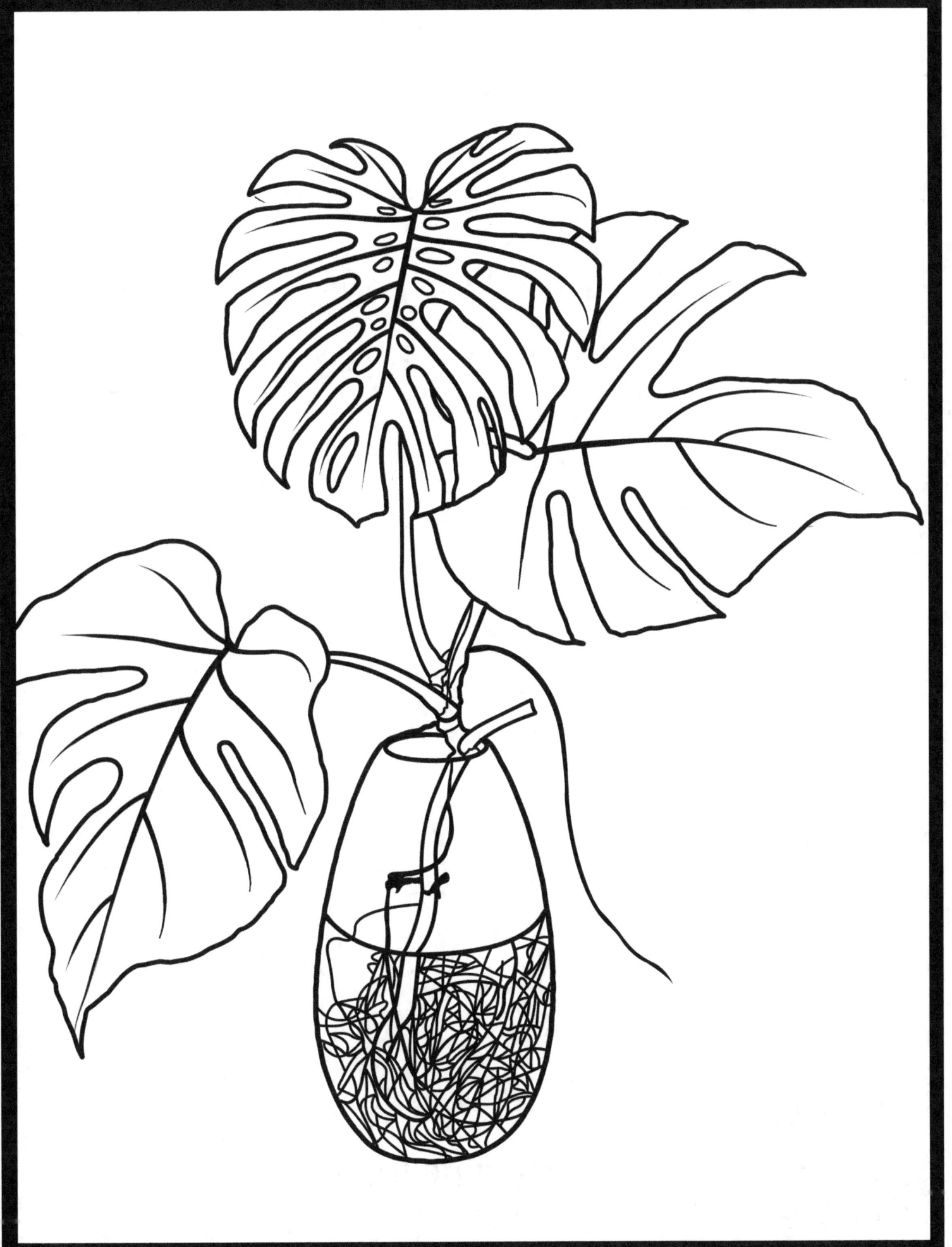

Monstera Deliciosa

www.crazyplantguy.com/gallery

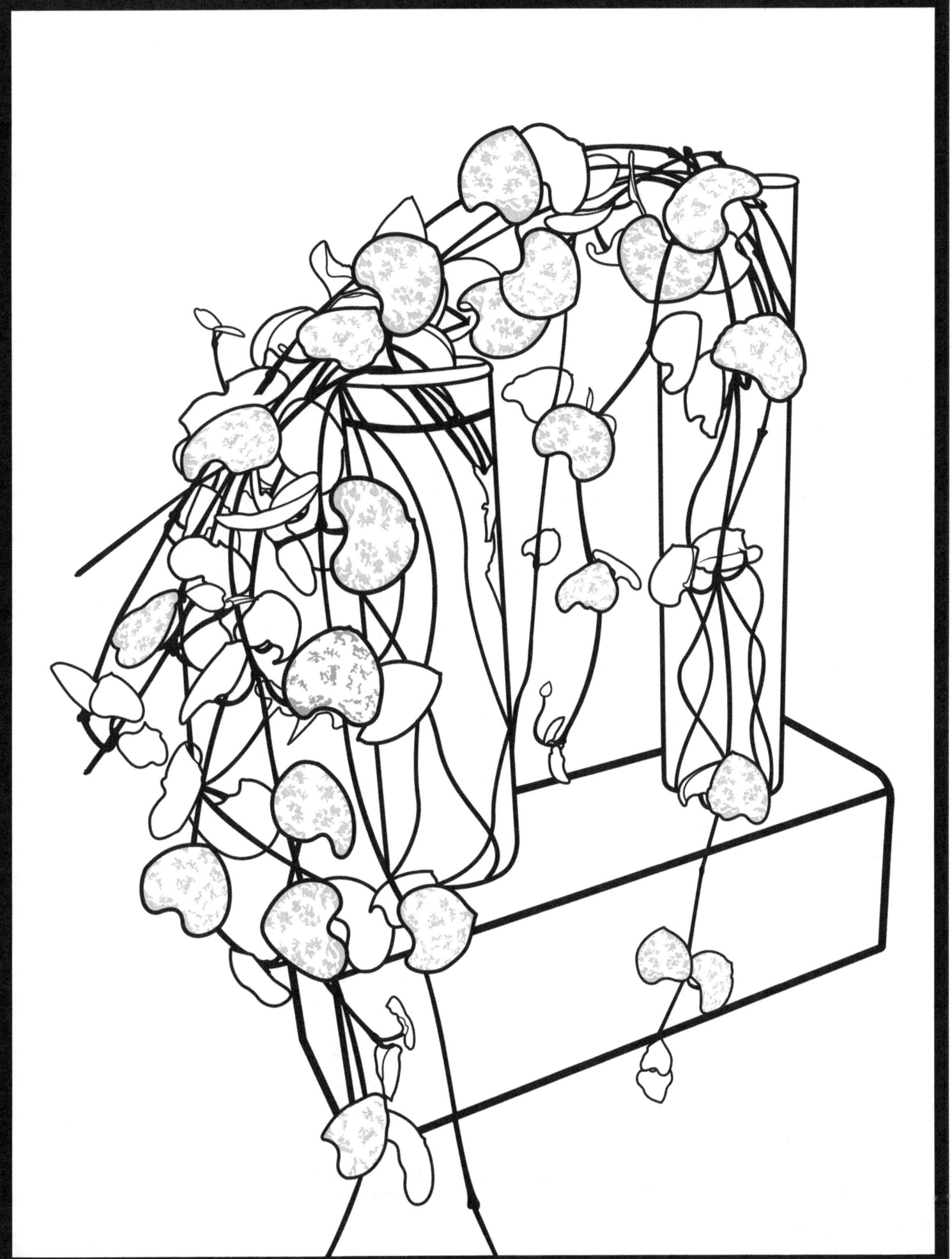

Variegated String of Hearts

www.crazyplantguy.com/gallery

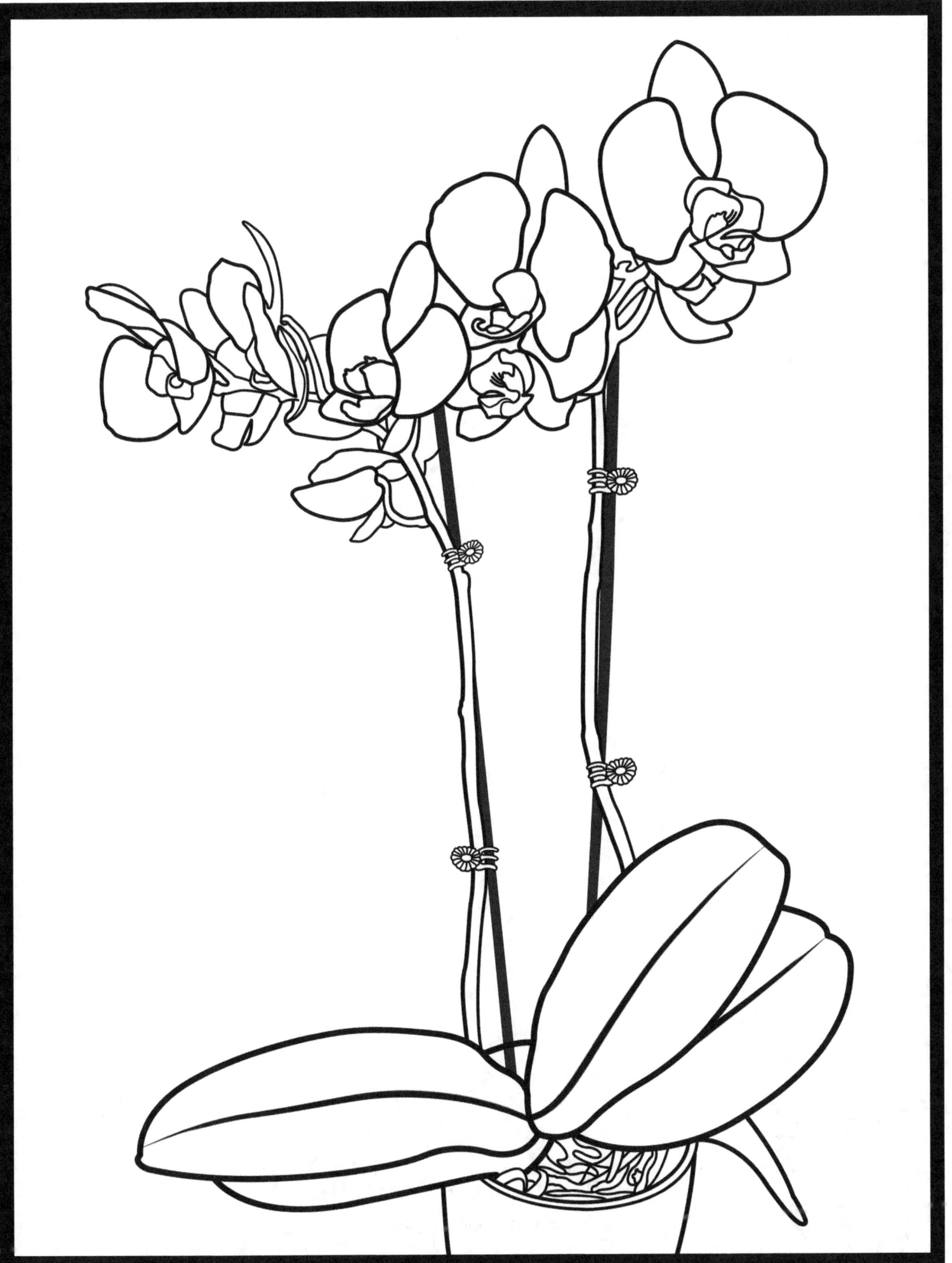

Phalaenopsis Orchid
www.crazyplantguy.com/gallery

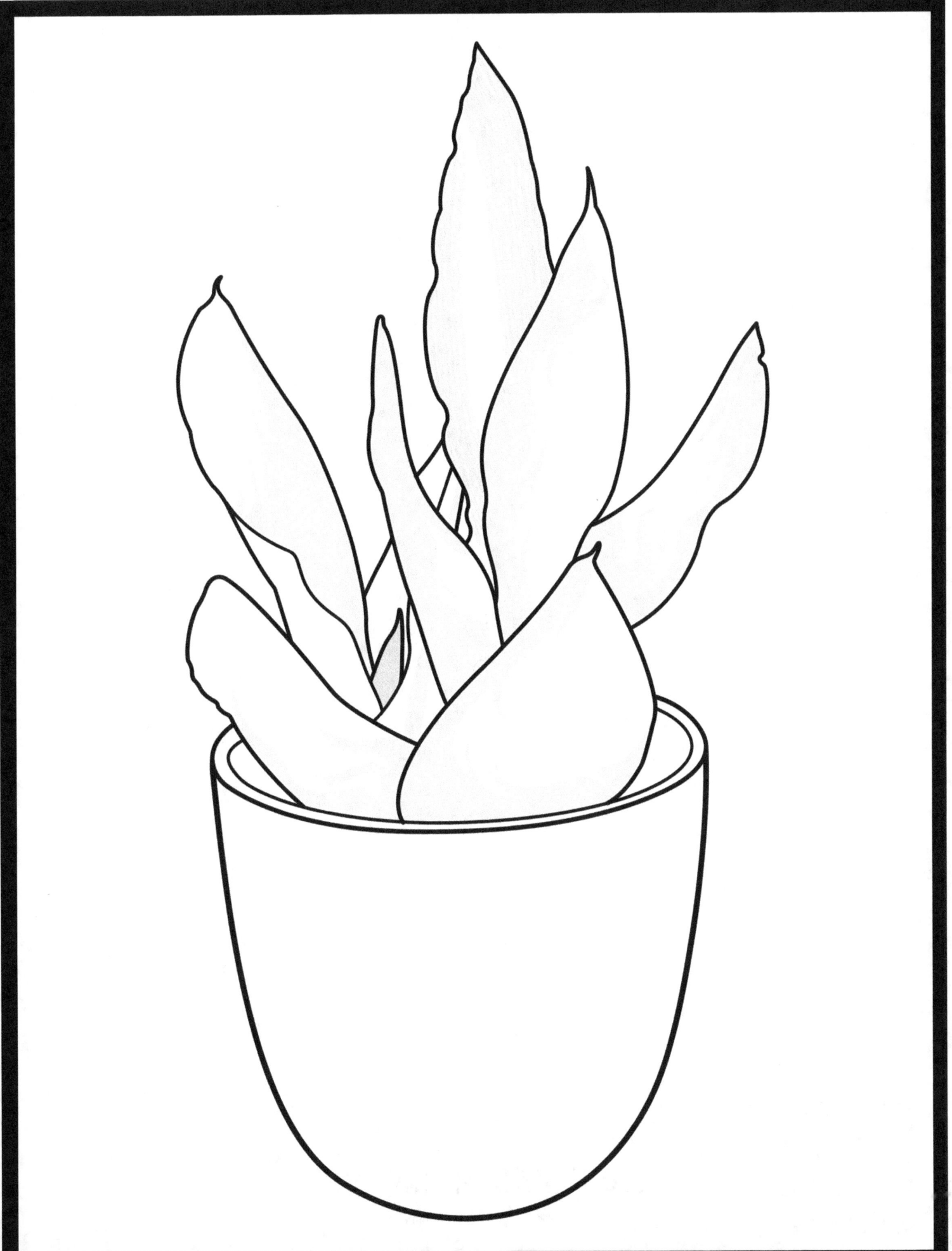

Moonshine Snake Plant

www.crazyplantguy.com/gallery

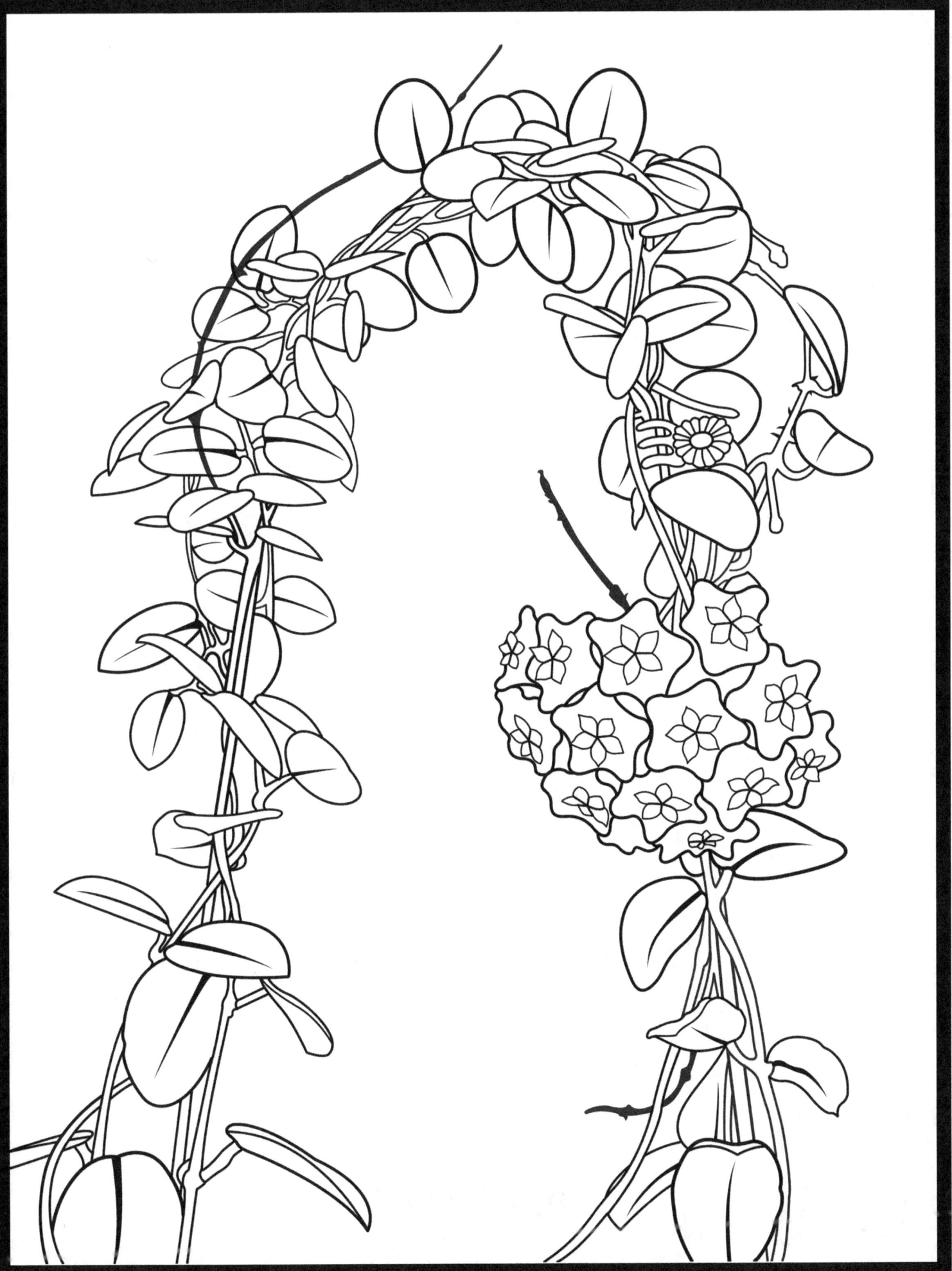

Hoya Mathilde

www.crazyplantguy.com/gallery

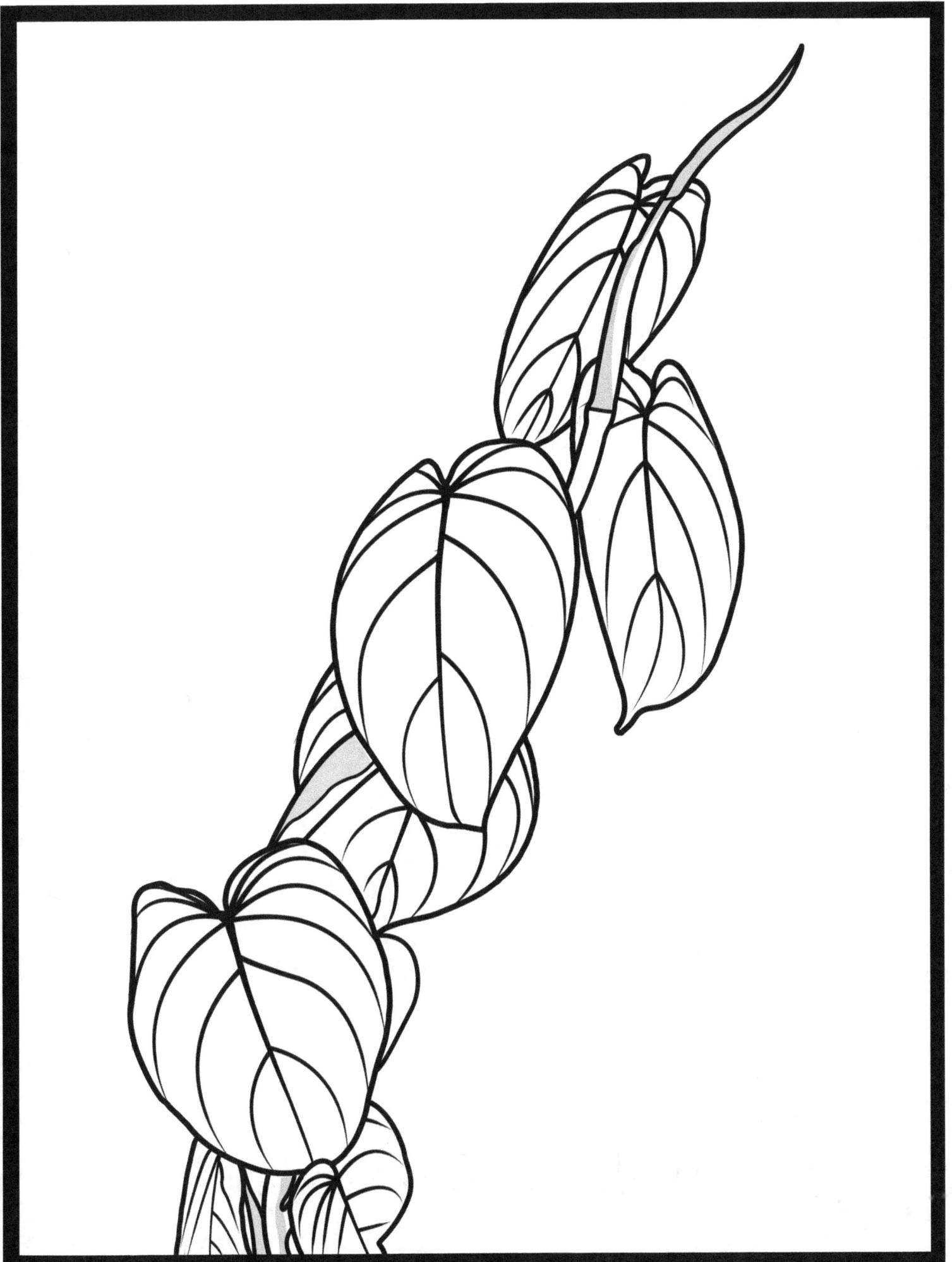

Philodendron Melanochrysum

www.crazyplantguy.com/gallery

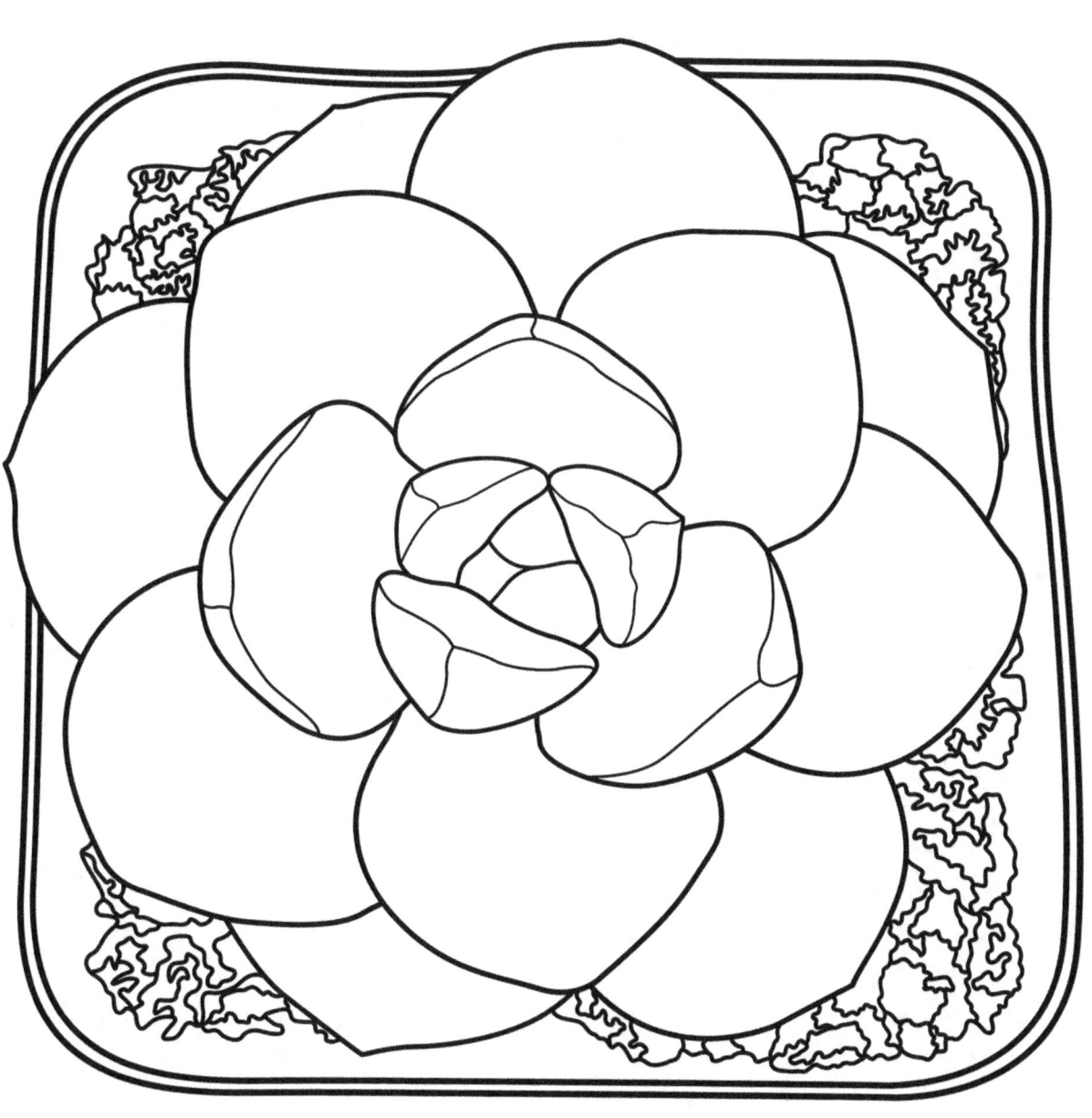

Echeveria Ice Green

www.crazyplantguy.com/gallery

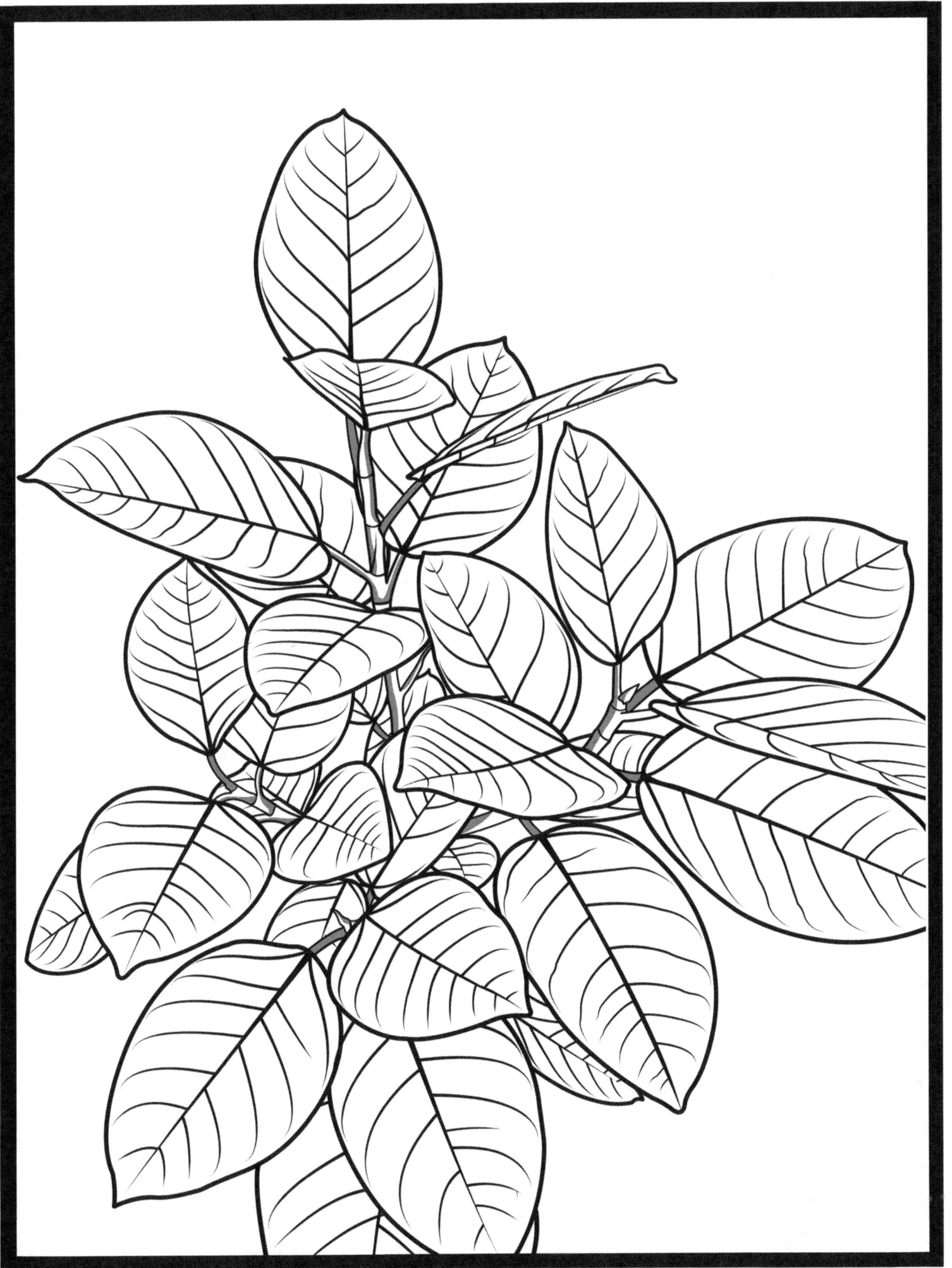

Ficus Altissima

www.crazyplantguy.com/gallery

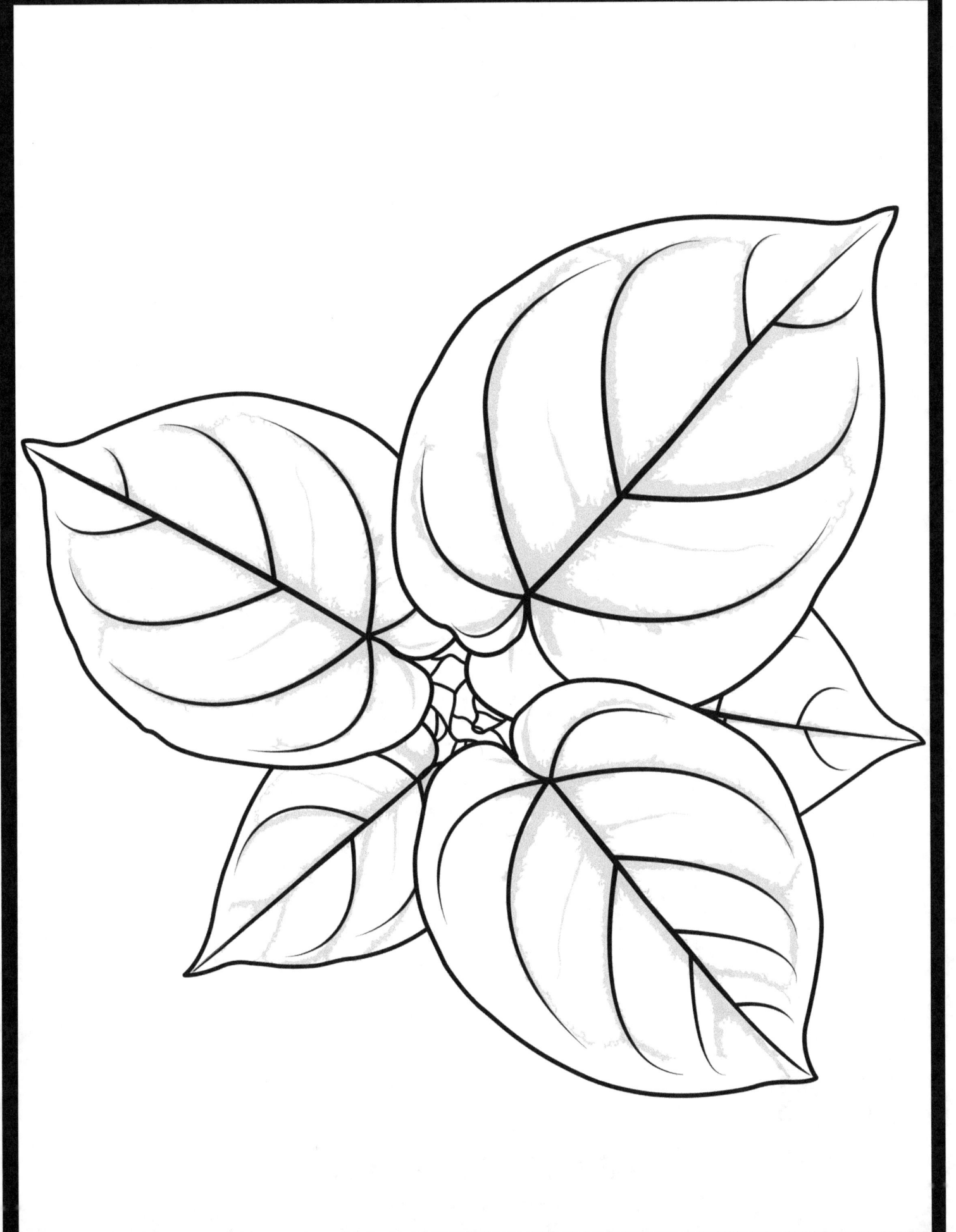

Anthurium Dorayaki

www.crazyplantguy.com/gallery

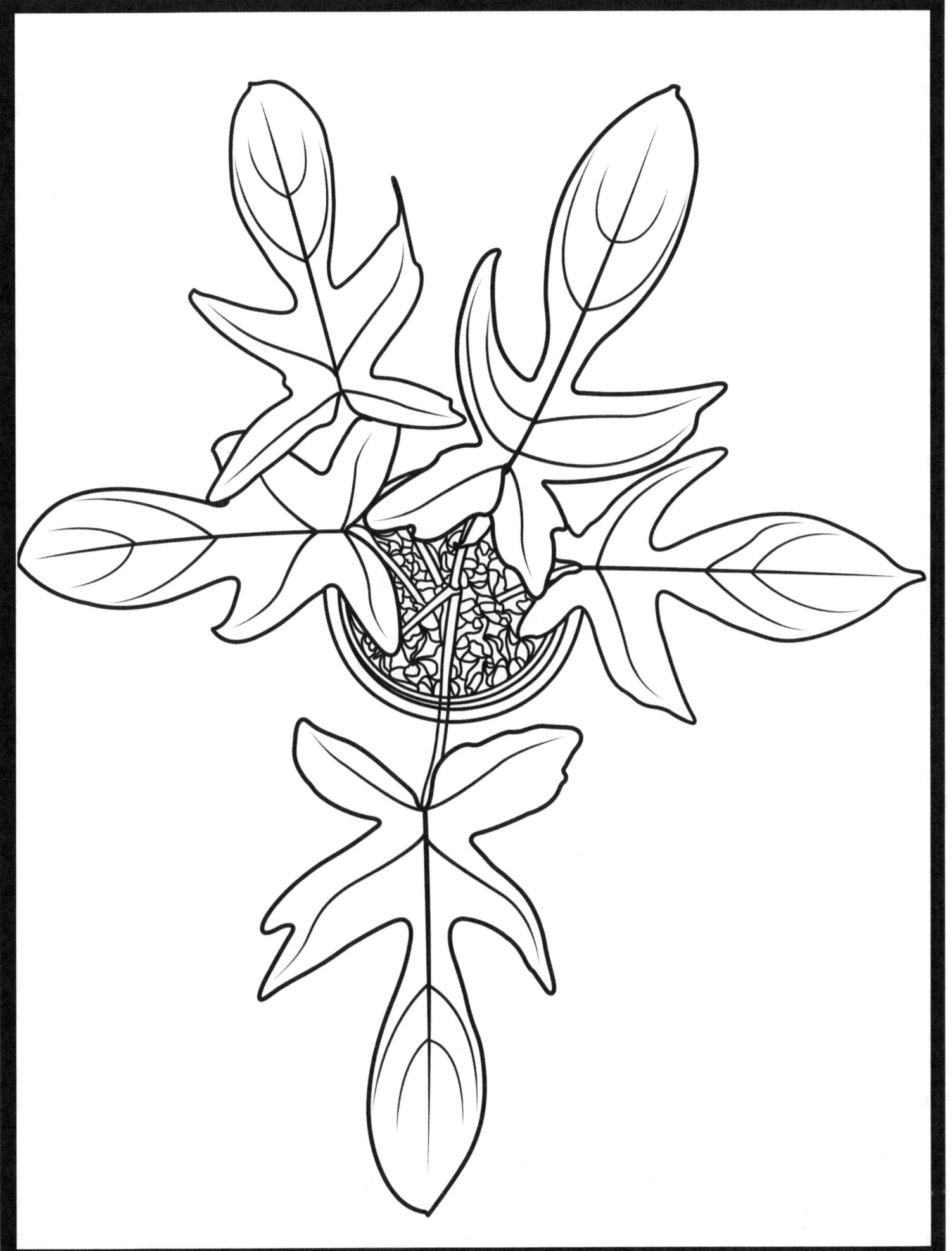

Philodendron Florida Ghost

www.crazyplantguy.com/gallery

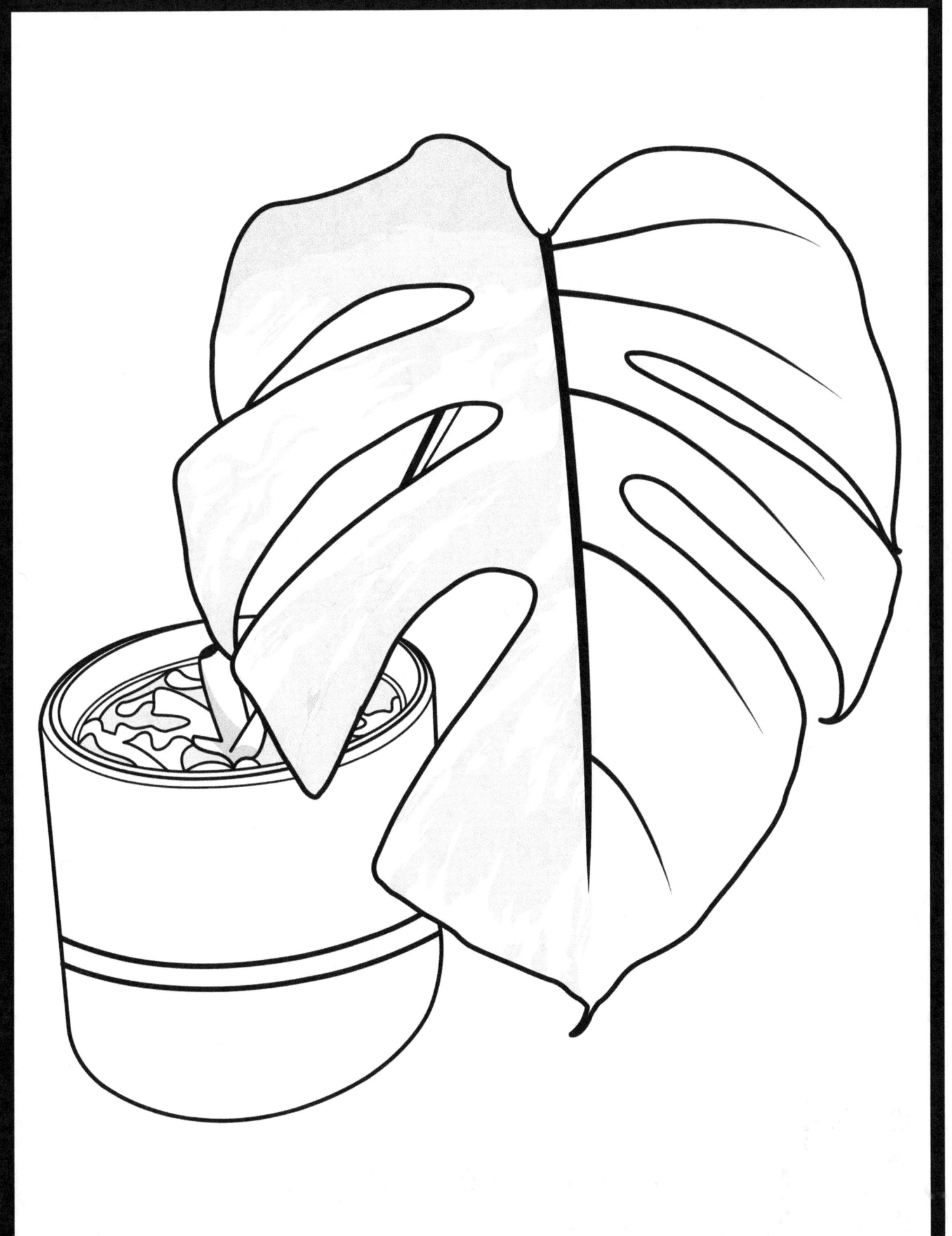

Monstera Albo Variegata

www.crazyplantguy.com/gallery

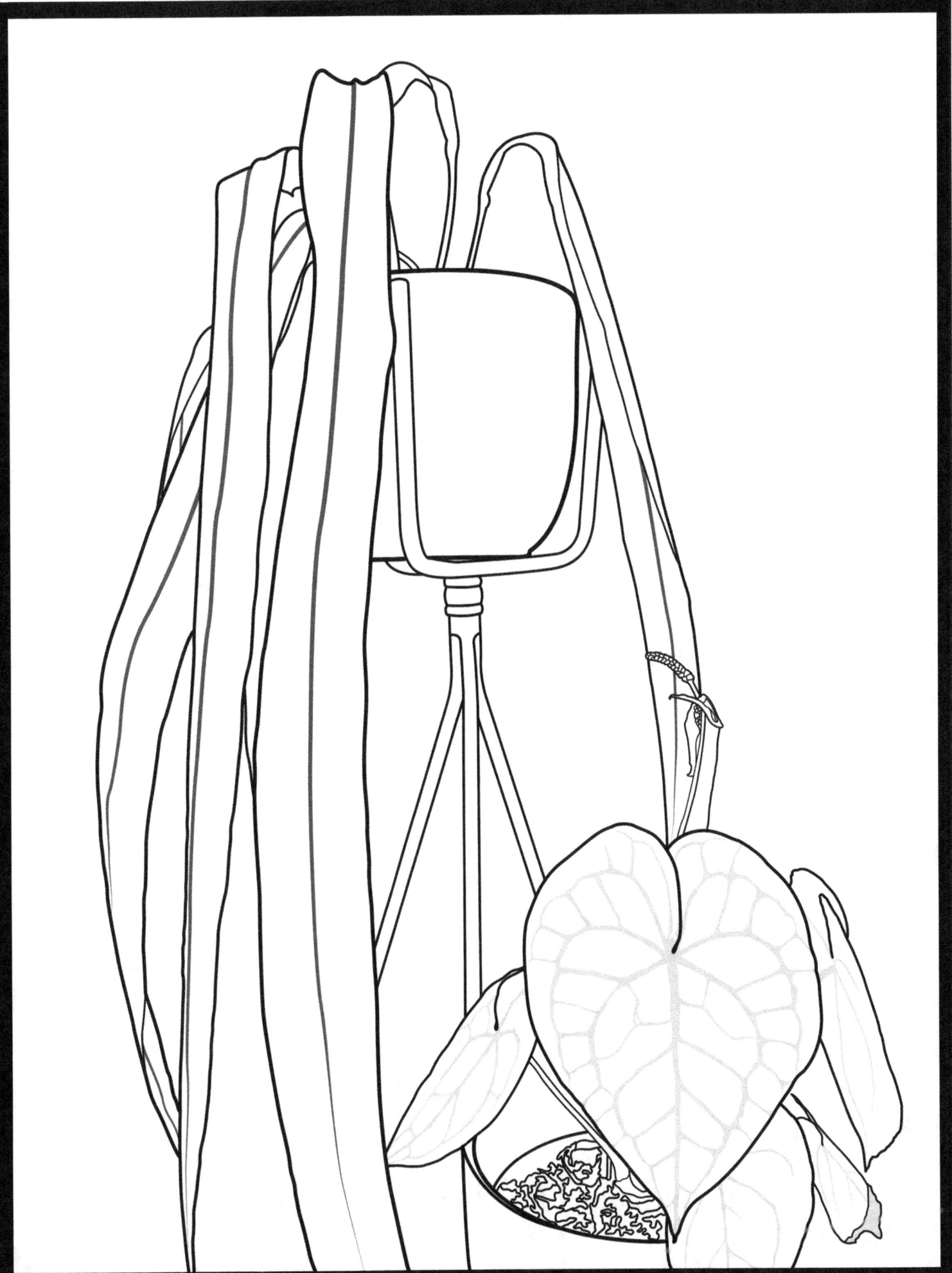

Anthurium Vittarifolium & Clarinervium

www.crazyplantguy.com/gallery

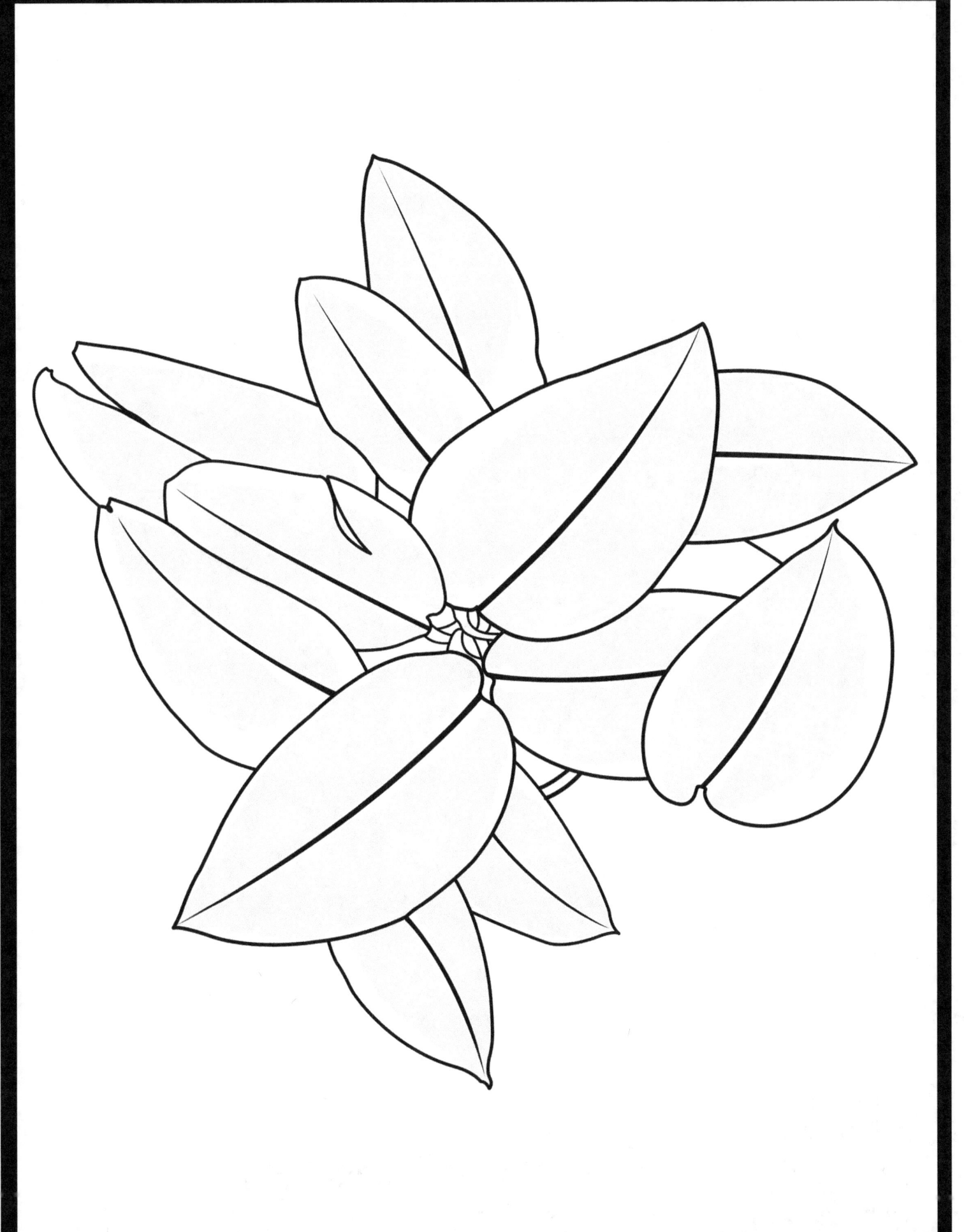

 **Scindapsus Treubii Moonlight**
www.crazyplantguy.com/gallery

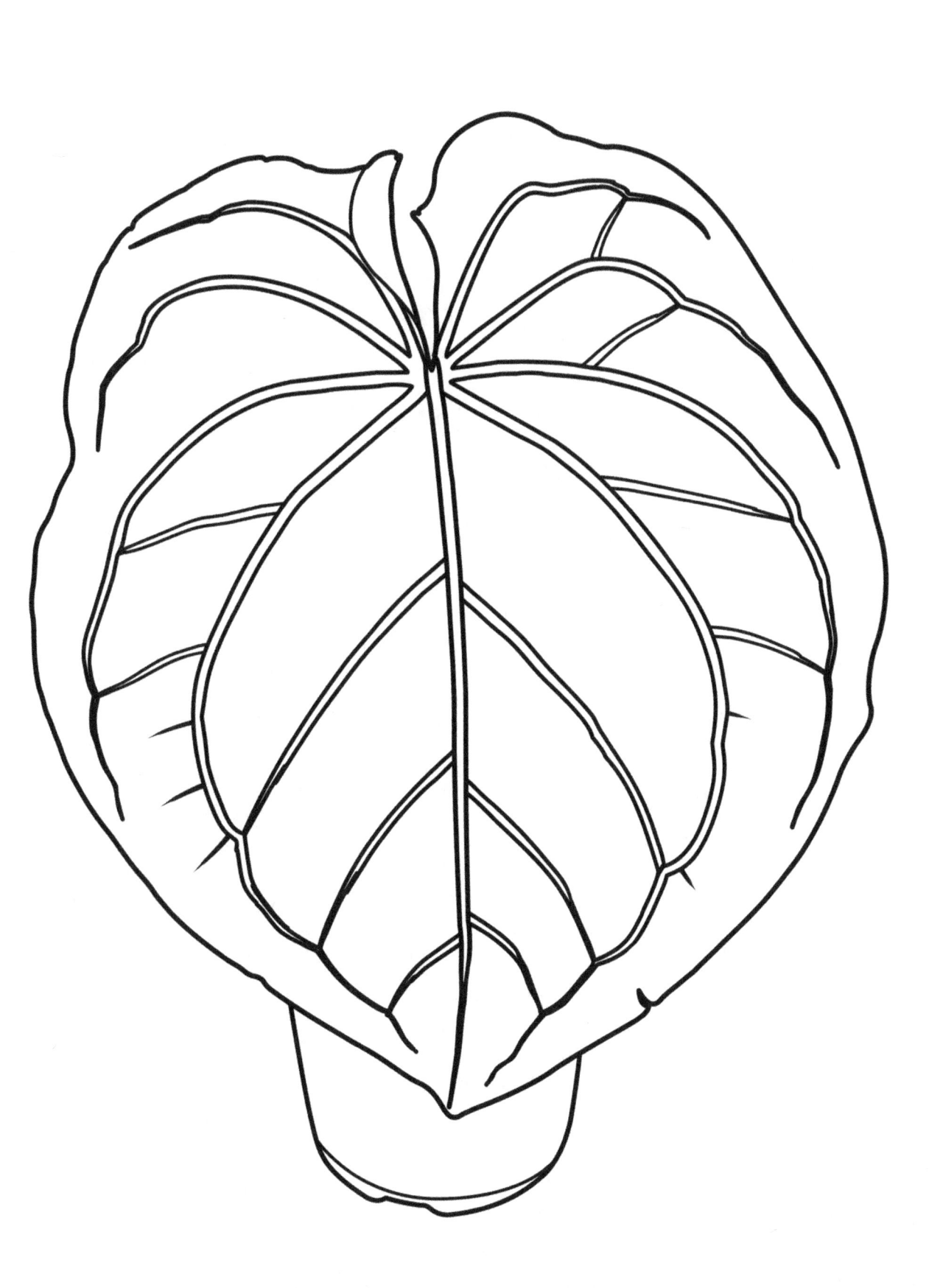

Anthurium Magnificum

www.crazyplantguy.com/gallery

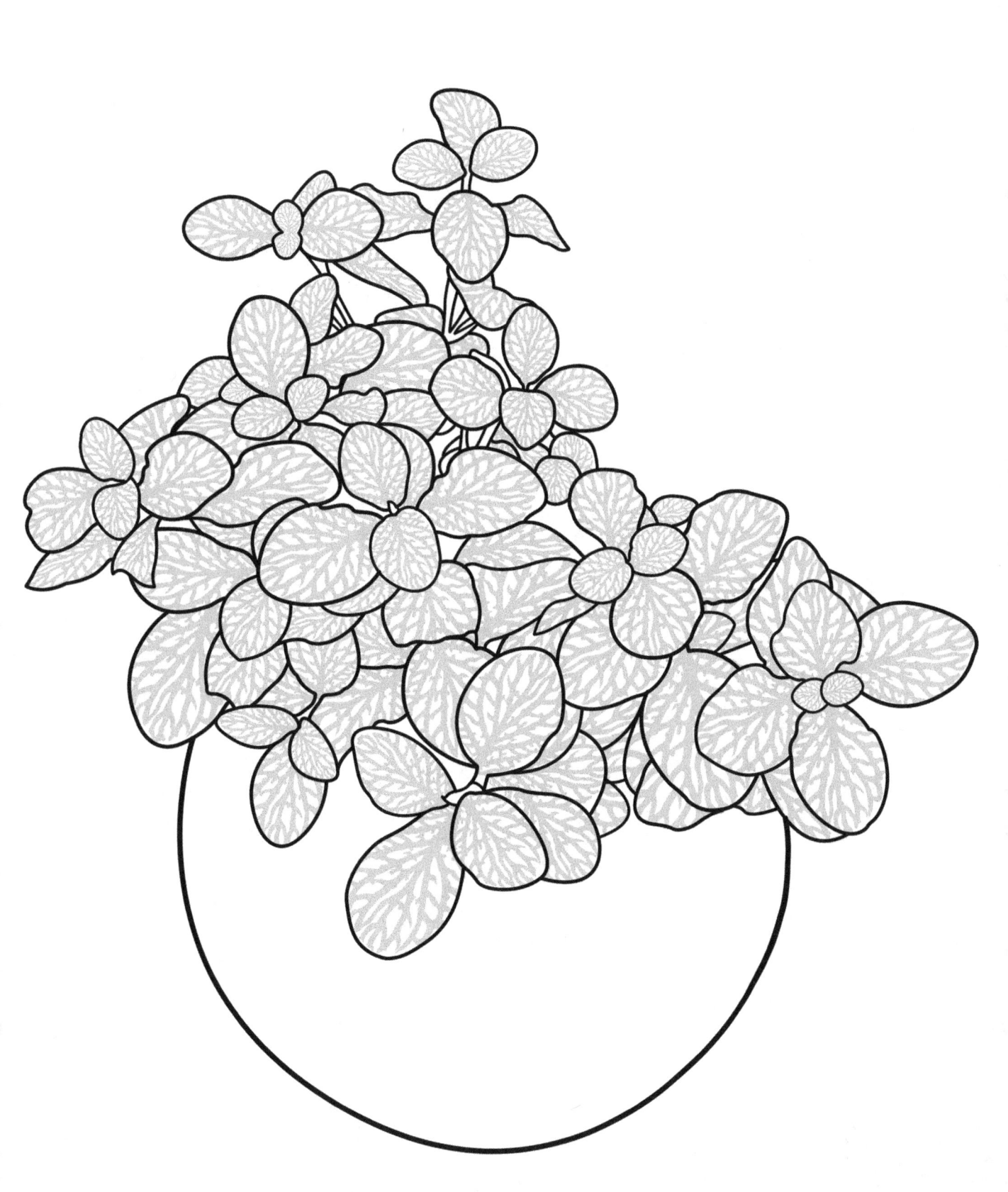

Fittonia Ruby Red

www.crazyplantguy.com/gallery

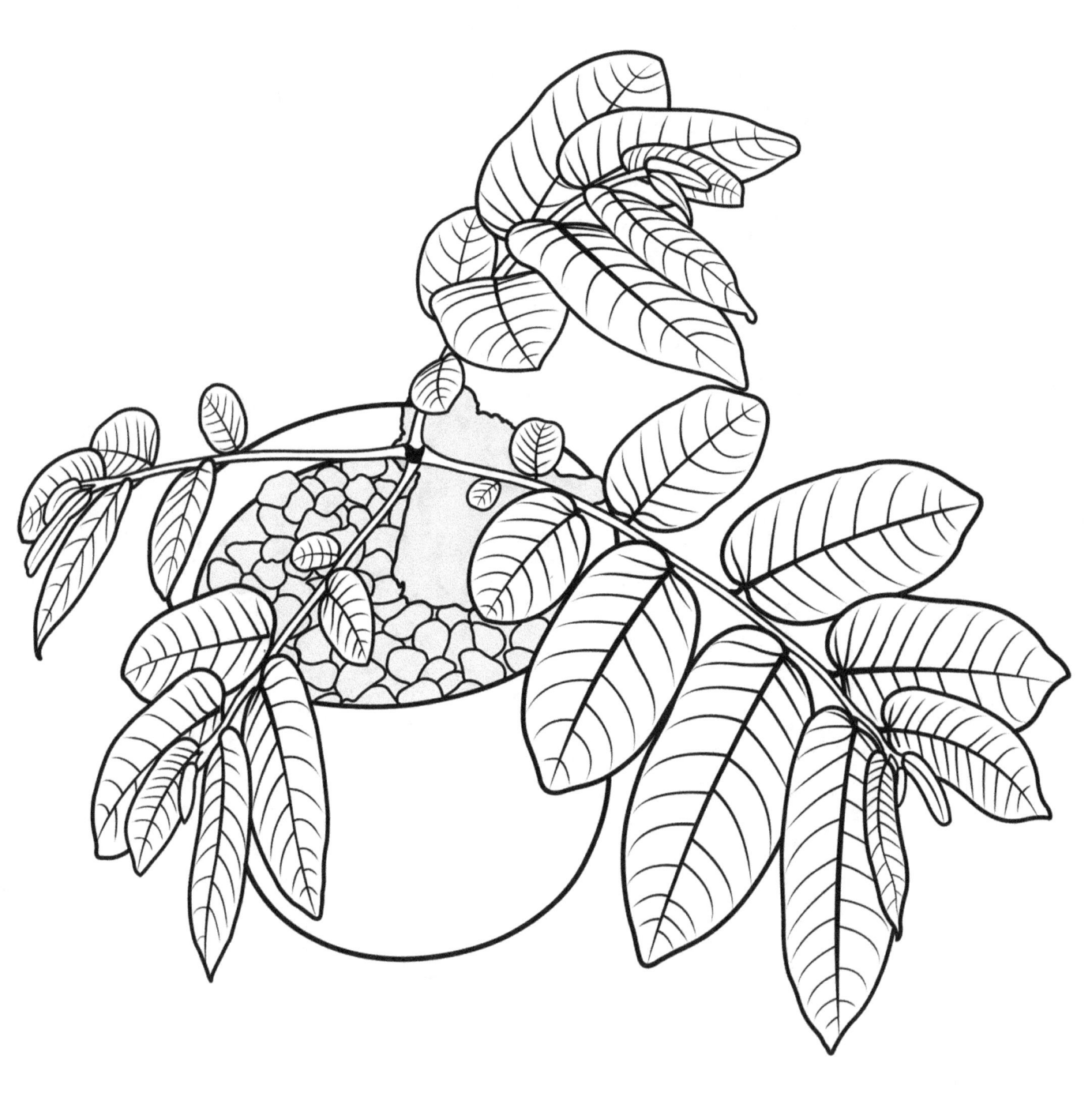

Phyllanthus Mirabilis - Dragon Wings

www.crazyplantguy.com/gallery

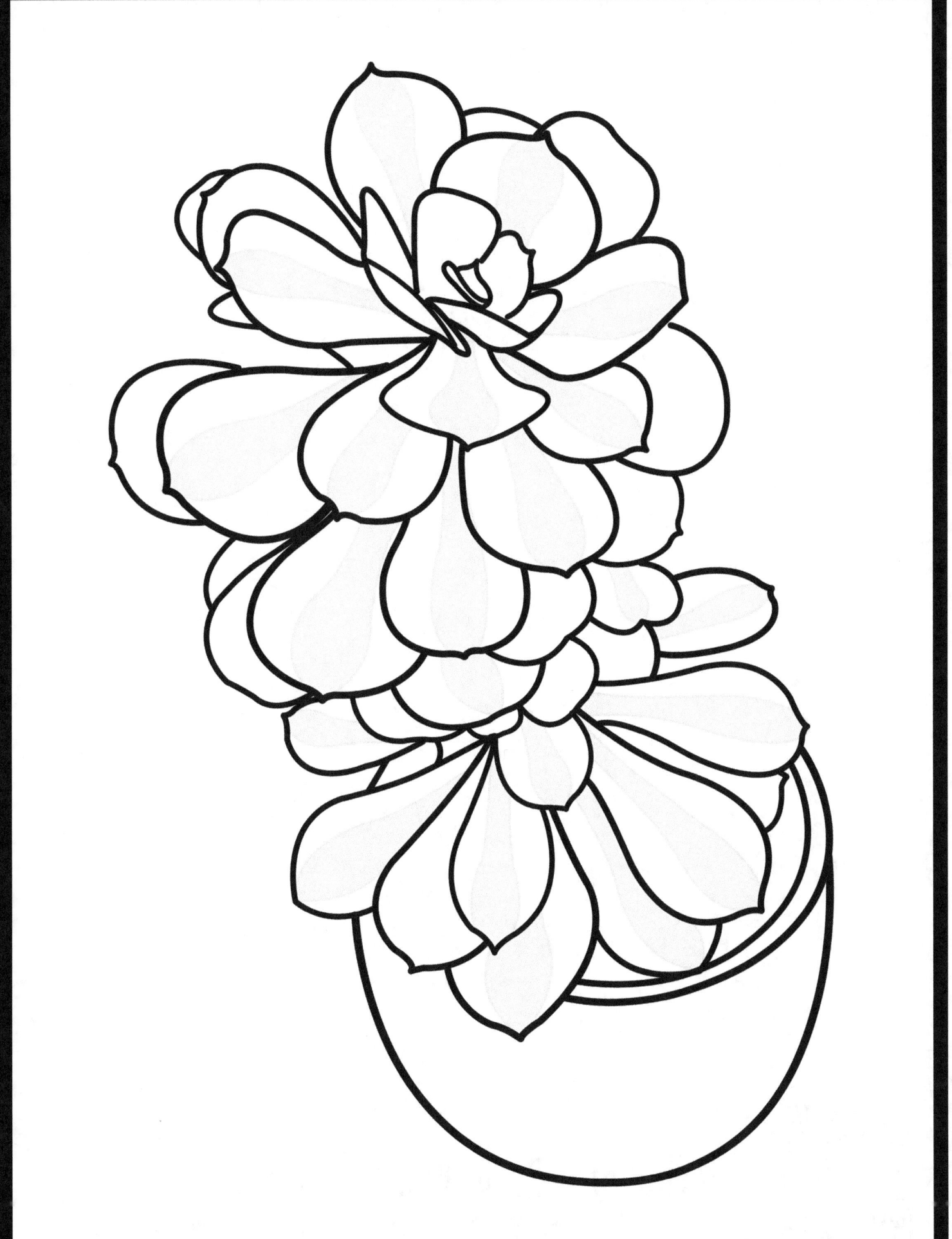

Echeveria Perle Von Nurnberg

www.crazyplantguy.com/gallery

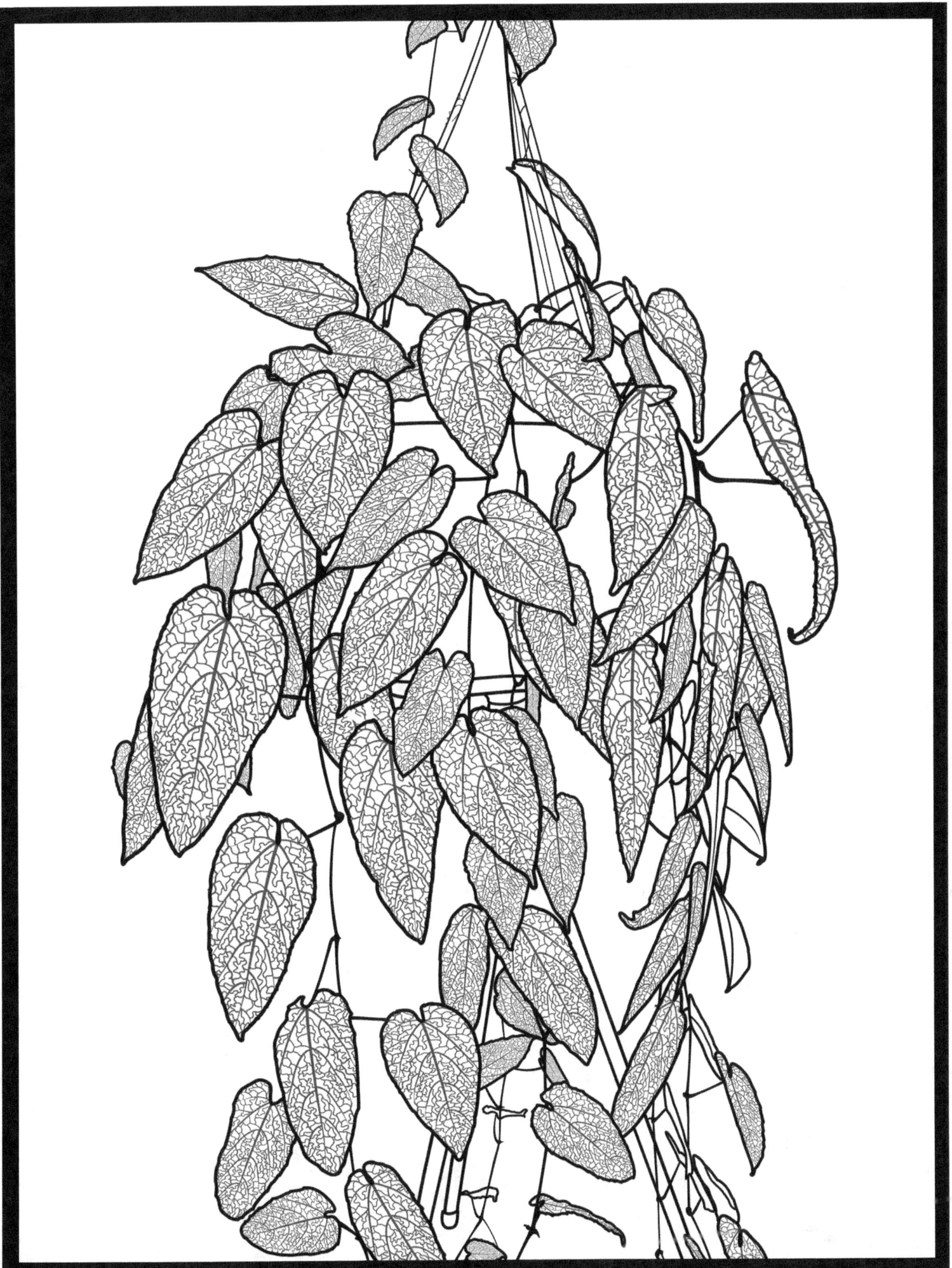

Cissus Discolor

www.crazyplantguy.com/gallery

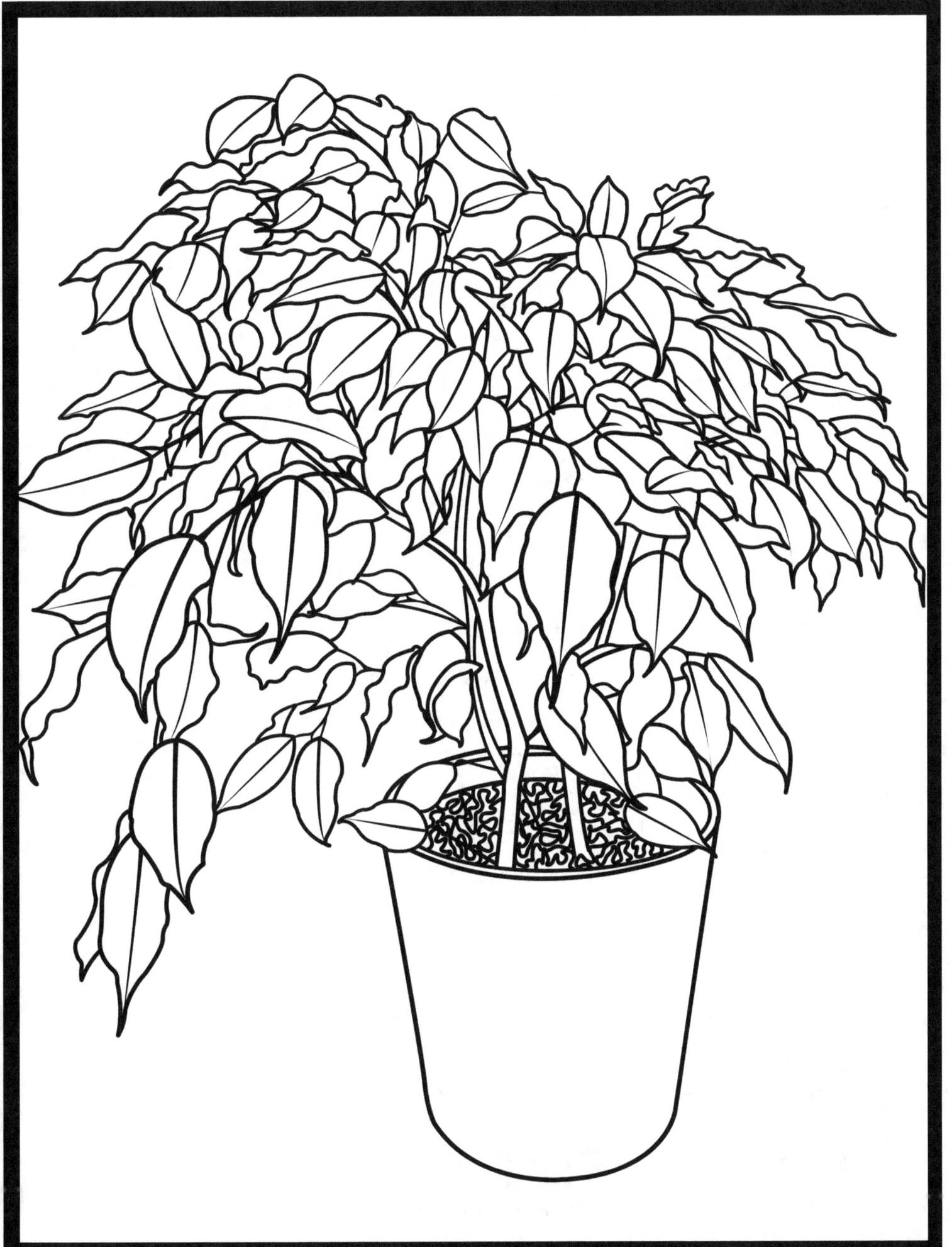

Ficus Benjamina

www.crazyplantguy.com/gallery

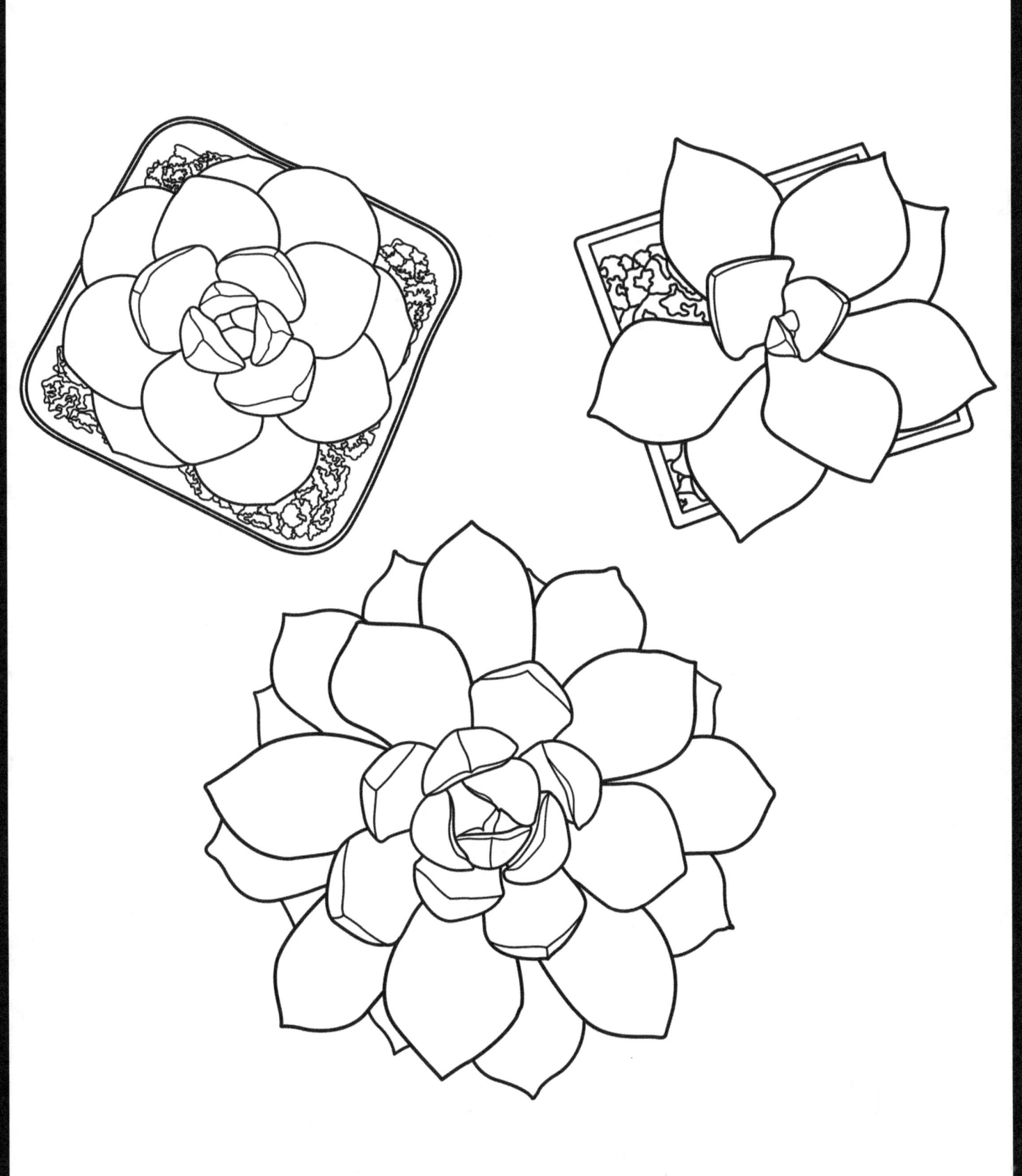

 Echeveria: Ice Green, Mrs. Richards, Snow Bunny

www.crazyplantguy.com/gallery

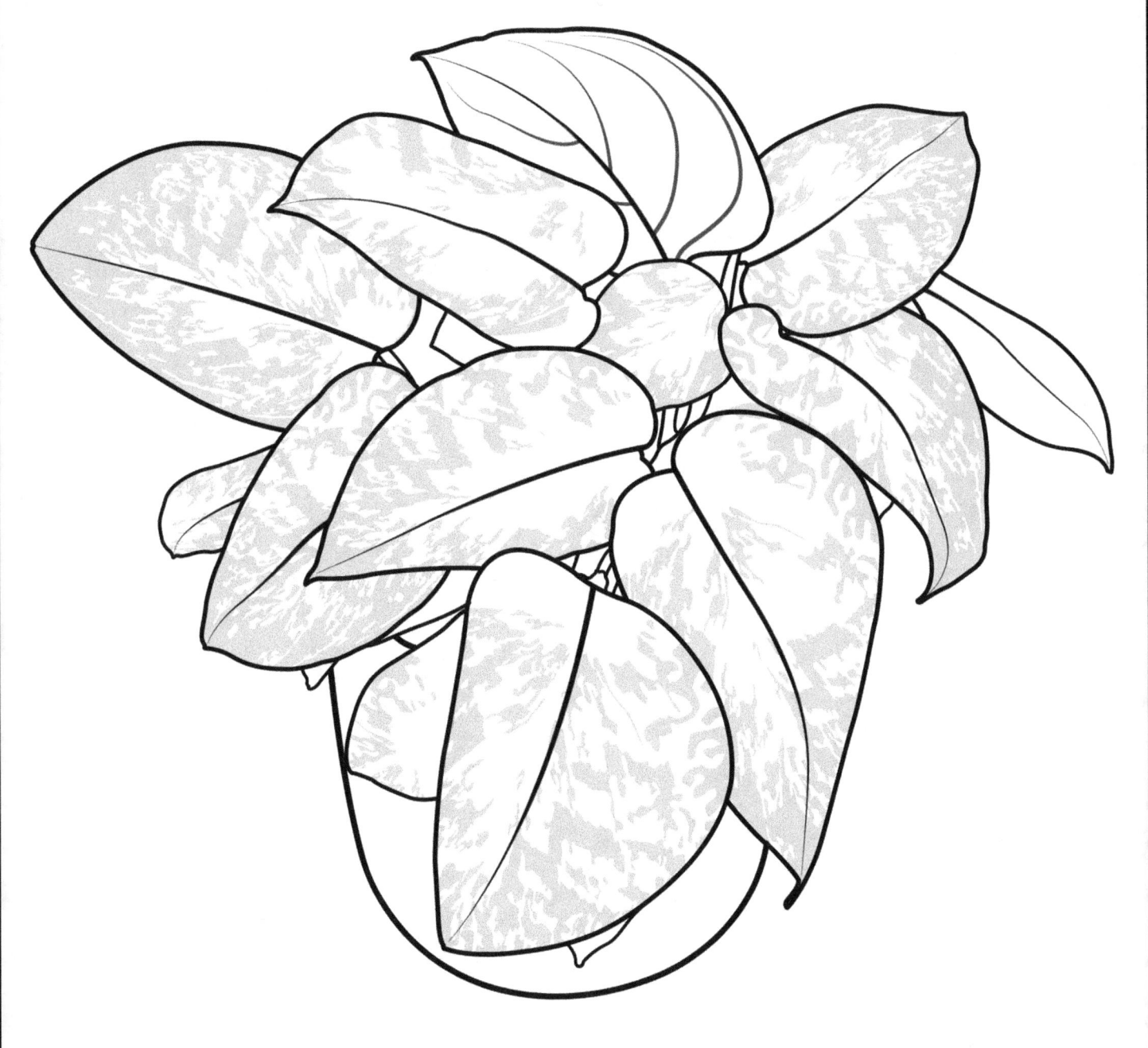

Scindapsus Pictus Silvery Ann

www.crazyplantguy.com/gallery

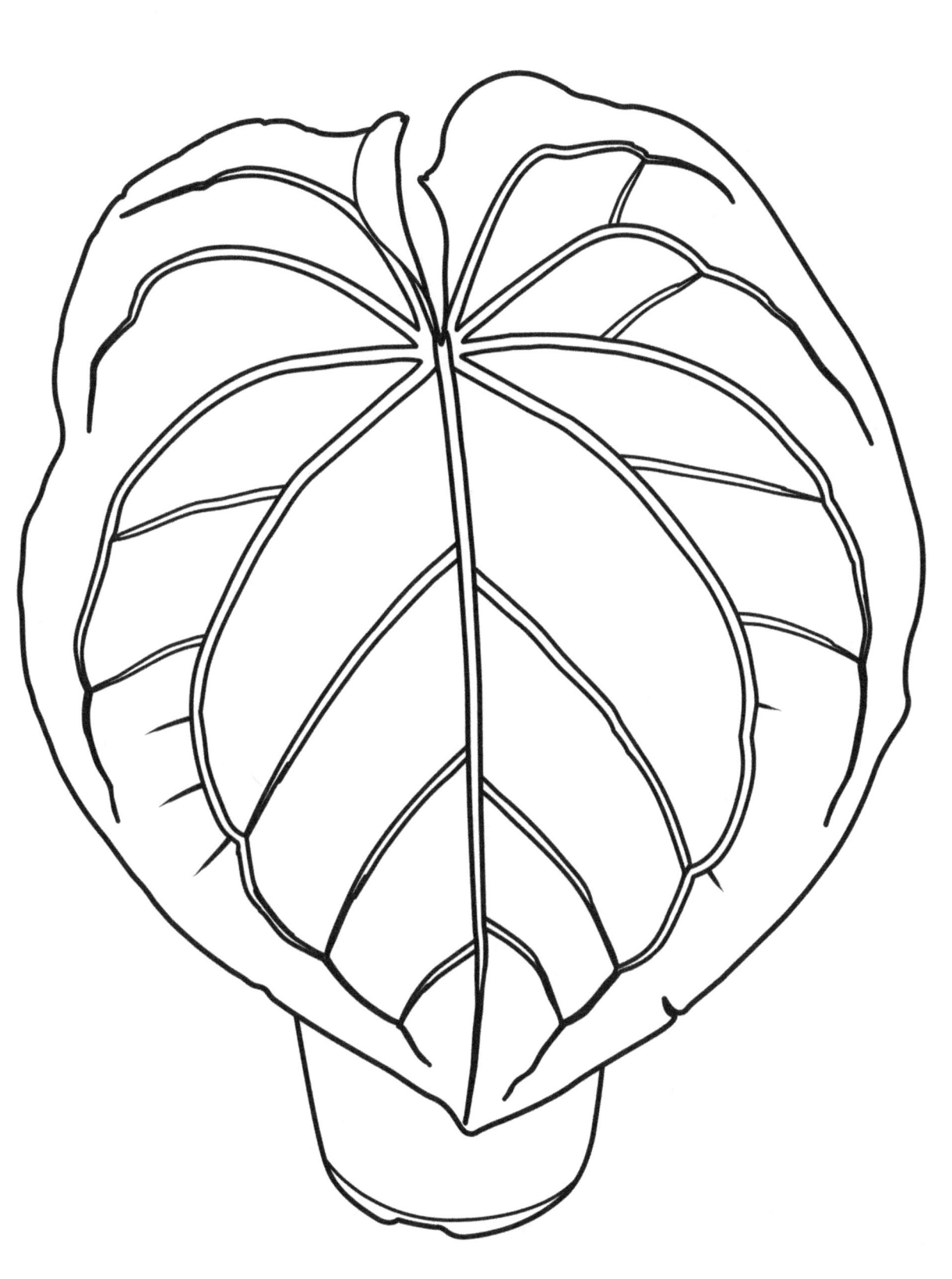

Anthurium Magnificum

www.crazyplantguy.com/gallery

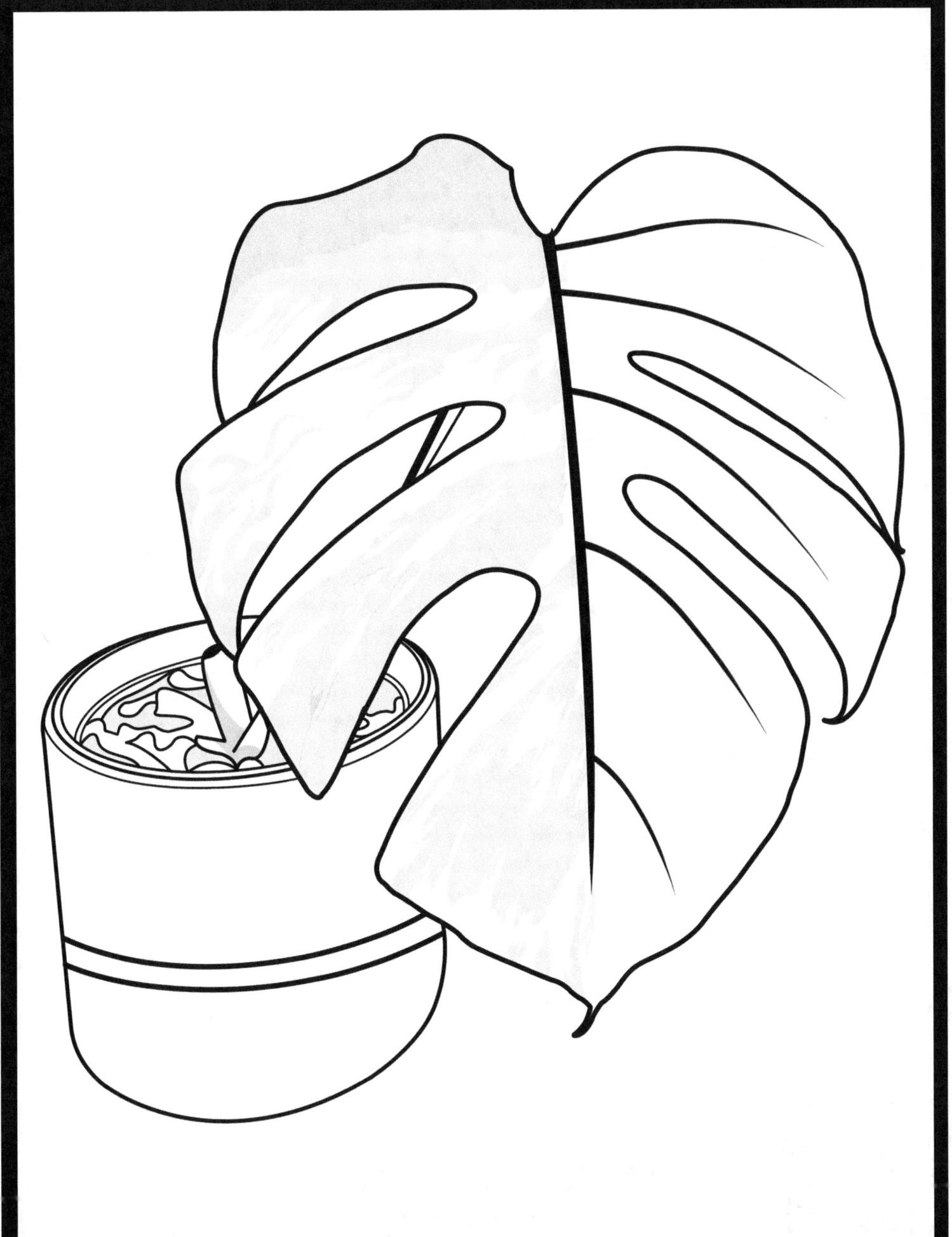

Monstera Albo Variegata

www.crazyplantguy.com/gallery

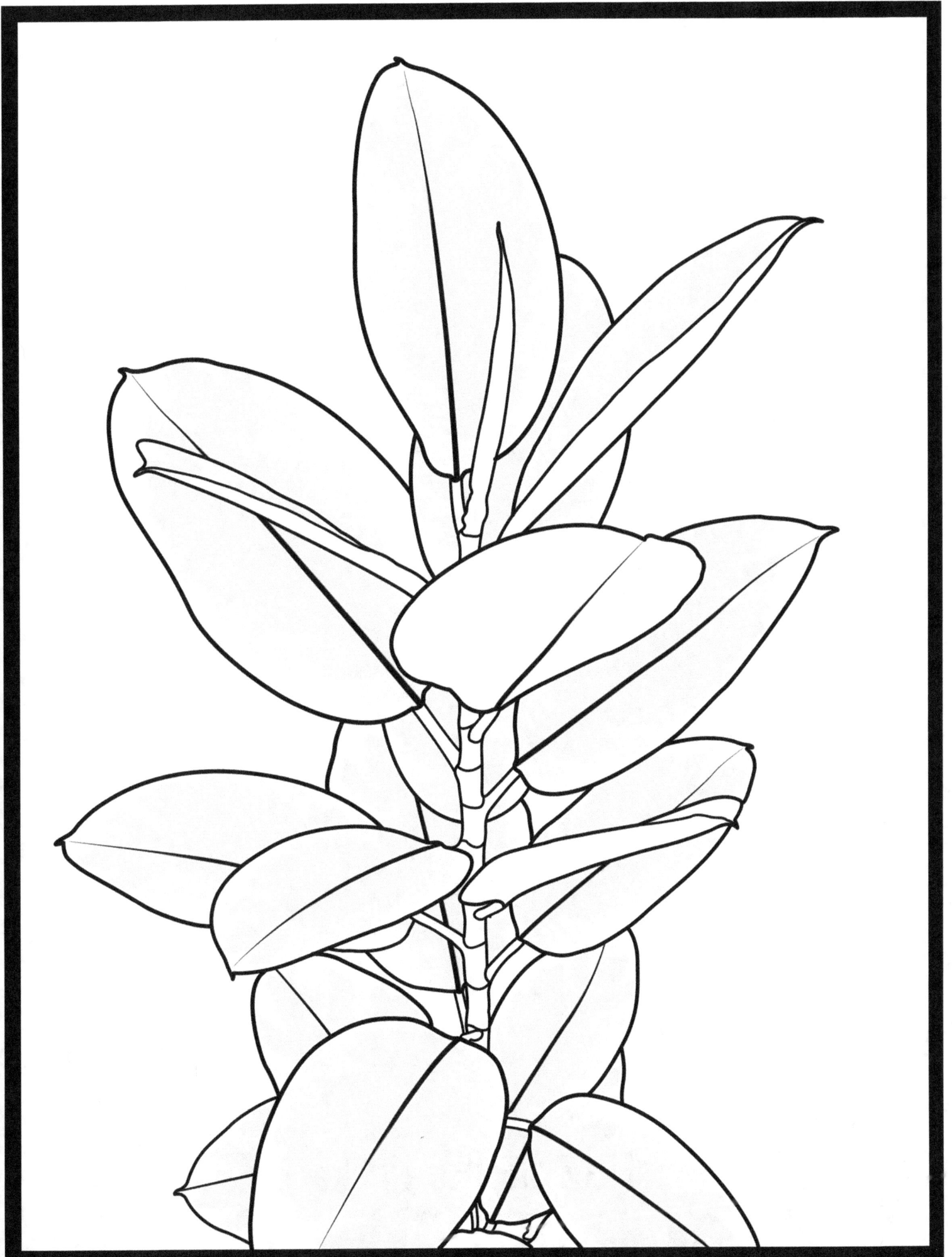

Ficus Elastica Tineke

www.crazyplantguy.com/gallery

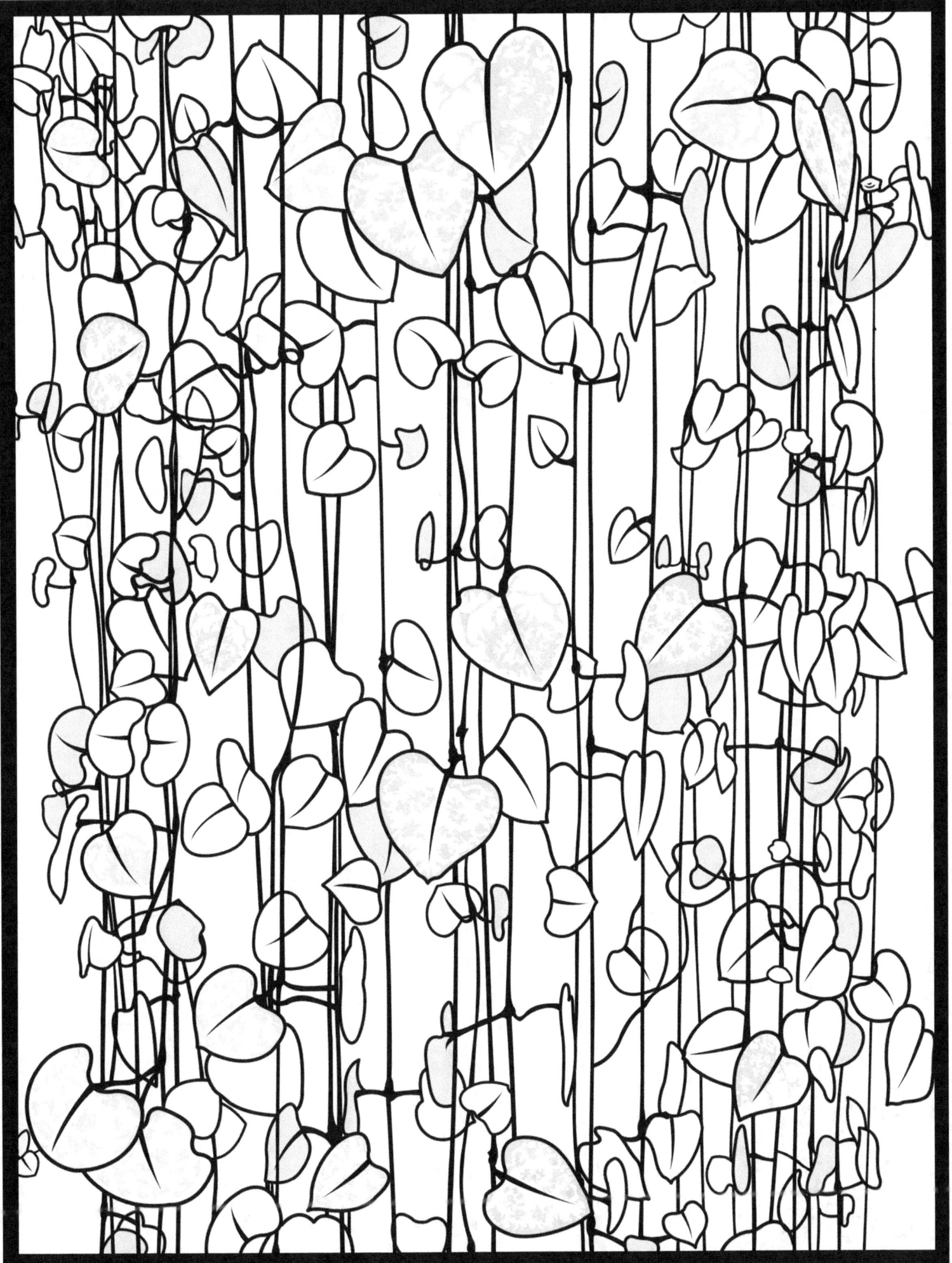

String of Hearts

www.crazyplantguy.com/gallery

www.ingramcontent.com/pod-product-compliance
Lightning Source LLC
Chambersburg PA
CBHW081437220526
45466CB00008B/2422